The Psychology of
The
Sopranos

*Boundaries and Boundary Violations in
Psychoanalysis* (with Eva P. Lester)

Psychiatry and the Cinema
(with Krin Gabbard)

*Psychodynamic Psychiatry
in Clinical Practice*

Psychoanalysis and Film

The Psychology of *The* Sopranos

Love, Death, Desire
and Betrayal in America's
Favorite Gangster Family

GLEN O. GABBARD, M.D.

BASIC
BOOKS

A Member of the Perseus Books Group

Published by Basic Books,
A Member of the Perseus Books Group

Library of Congress Cataloging-in-Publication Data
Gabbard, Glen O.
The psychology of The Sopranos : love, death, desire and betrayal in
America's favorite gangster family / Glen O. Gabbard
        p. cm.
ISBN 0-465-02735-0
    1. Sopranos (Television program)   I. Title.
PN1992.77.S66 G33 2002
791.45'72—dc21

                                                          2002004404

Text design by Jeffrey P. Williams
Set in 10.5 Berling by the Perseus Books Group

First Edition

02   03   04 / 10   9   8   7   6   5   4   3   2   1

To my fellow Bada Bingers

Phil ∘ Peggy ∘ Joel ∘ Jodi ∘ Joyce ∘ Sharon ∘ Frank
Mike ∘ Stuart ∘ Amanda ∘ Abigail ∘ Keith

"It is, it is a glorious thing to be a Pirate King."

GILBERT AND SULLIVAN,
The Pirates of Penzance

CONTENTS

PREFACE

WHEN FRIENDS AND COLLEAGUES hear that I've written a book about *The Sopranos*, some respond with comments like: "Hey, it's only a TV show—aren't you taking this a bit too seriously?" And "Why don't you get a life?" My answers are, respectively, "Probably," and "I'm looking for one." But these detractors are not fellow *Sopranos* fanatics. My kindred spirits fully understand my passion.

David Chase and his gifted group of writers have created a tragicomic universe that, while at times side-splittingly funny, is not always pretty. As T. S. Eliot reminds us, "human kind cannot bear very much reality," a philosophy apparently shared by the four networks that turned down *The Sopranos* before Home Box Office snapped it up. In an age when even "reality TV" bears little resemblance to real life, Chase and HBO have chosen to defy network conventions and deliver a television show that brilliantly illuminates what it means to be human. Their refreshing version of reality has tapped into an audience of people who are not habitual TV viewers, let alone cable subscribers. They appreciate the show's sharp wit, Machiavellian plot turns and Shakespearean character development. Indeed, as the book's subtitle suggests, viewers resonate with the existential dilemmas—of love, death, desire and betrayal—so vividly showcased in this well-crafted drama.

In this book I take a hard, but lighthearted, look at those dilemmas as they reveal themselves in the psyches of America's favorite Mob family—and our own. I explore what *The Sopranos* teaches us about psychology and psychotherapy, and I offer my thoughts about why we are drawn to a series about the misadventures of a middle-aged thug. Although presumably most of us are not connected with organized crime, remarkably we seem to find ourselves reflected in the members of Tony Soprano's two families. The writers and cast deserve tremendous credit for deftly leading us to self-recognition through the lives of New Jersey outlaws.

As a psychoanalyst, I've long been fascinated by how psychotherapy is portrayed in film and on TV (I've indulged this interest in my book *Psychiatry and the Cinema*). The degree of psychiatric realism in *The Sopranos* is unprecedented—once one accepts the conceit of mobster-as-patient. In fact, I fear Chase and his colleagues have blown our cover. They've lifted the veil on the secret world of psychotherapy—and, happily, viewers love what they see.

I have many people to thank for helping me complete this book in time for the beginning of the fourth season of *The Sopranos*. My agent, Rafe Sagalyn, encouraged me to write the book at the end of the third season. Jo Ann Miller, my marvelous editor at Basic Books, forced me at "virtual" gunpoint to eliminate all traces of psychoanalytic jargon from my prose. She helped me accept the radical notion that readers would enjoy English more than psychobabble. Jo Ann's able assistant, Candace Taylor, also deserves special thanks for the extensive work she did on all aspects of the project. My friend and colleague Frank Sacco read much of the manuscript and gave me a greater appreciation of the cultural ambience in which *The Sopranos* takes place. I also want to express my appreciation to Faye Schoenfeld, who conscientiously typed early drafts of the book, and Diane Clay, my assistant at Baylor College of Medicine, who typed last-minute revisions and helped me keep my sanity under the pressure of relentless deadlines.

I owe a special debt of gratitude to members of *The Sopranos* family. Over many months of long conversations, Robin Green and Mitchell Burgess, Emmy Award–winning writers and executive producers of the series, gave me an invaluable insider's perspective on the show. Felicia Lipchik graciously provided me with videotapes so I could view episodes again and again. Ronald Green, professor of psychiatry at Dartmouth School of Medicine, and the show's unofficial psychiatric consultant, told me wonderful stories of how he helped create the psychotherapy scenes.

The Psychology of The Sopranos may appear to have one author, but it was most definitely a team effort. To anyone who thinks this kind of book can be written without generous allies, I can only say, "Fuhgedaboudit."

....

BADA BEING AND NOTHINGNESS

THE DOOR TO A PSYCHIATRIST'S OFFICE opens into the waiting room. A 40-something female psychiatrist hobbles out on crutches, and the young female patient looks at the cast on her leg with concern. She follows her doctor into the office and sits across from her. After a few seconds of uncomfortable silence, the patient asks her therapist, "Should you really be here?"

The psychiatrist responds, "I feel better when I'm working."

The patient pauses for a moment and asks, "You mean, like Dr. Melfi?"

This real-life account of a therapy session reflects how David Chase's spectacularly successful Home Box Office (HBO) series, *The Sopranos,* has entered into our collective consciousness. Here the patient is referring to Dr. Jennifer

Melfi's rapid return to her consulting room after being raped in a parking garage. In another therapy session, a thousand miles away from the first, a female analyst is upbraided by her patient for walking down an isolated stairwell to a parking garage. Her angry patient shouts at her, "That's where Dr. Melfi was raped!"

The Sopranos has received unprecedented praise from media critics. Writing in the *Nation*, Ellen Willis referred to it as "the richest and most compelling piece of television—no, of popular culture—that I've encountered in the past twenty years." Television critic Nancy Franklin notes, "There has certainly never been anything like it on TV, and on network TV there never *could* be anything like it—it goes out on a limb that doesn't even exist at the networks." In its third season the show received the highest ratings in HBO's history for a non-sporting event. Perhaps most telling, in 2001, huge numbers of Academy Awards watchers switched over in the middle of the annual event to get their weekly Sunday evening fix of *The Sopranos*.

Indeed, in towns and cities all over the United States and Europe, there is a "*Sopranos* effect" on the evening of a new episode. Retail establishments are suddenly deserted. Restaurant patrons make a hasty exit. Social invitations are declined. Answering machines pick up phone calls so not a single word of dialogue is missed.

The human condition involves psychological conflict, the inevitability of strife in intimate relationships, existential loneliness and crises of meaning. These psychological struggles are writ larger than life each week on *The Sopranos*, and we are drawn to the show because of them. In this book, I explore human psychology as it unfolds in *The Sopranos*, not only in the context of psychotherapy but in the characters' relationships, behavior and dreams that occur outside the consulting room. The series' writers, clearly serious students of human behavior, have done what Hamlet recommended to a troupe of traveling players visiting Elsinore. They have held a mirror up to nature—human nature, that is—and 11 million viewers can't take their eyes off the reflection.

Psychotherapists have shown a particular interest in *The Sopranos*. Many of them hooked up to cable or subscribed to HBO solely to see Jennifer Melfi's latest session with mobster Tony Soprano. And the next day over coffee or in the elevator, they critique Melfi's therapeutic strategies, chortle over Tony's malapropisms (Hannibal "Lecture" is one of my favorites), argue vehemently about whether or not Tony is treatable, express their growing distress about Dr. Melfi's crossing her legs when she wears a short skirt; and they debate Tony's diagnosis and micromanage Melfi's medication choices. These informal discussions were formalized in the third season when three other psychoanalysts and I began discussing each episode on the slate.com TV Club. The *Slate* discussion became popular beyond the wildest expectations of its editors, with hundreds of thousands of readers regularly following our dialogue.

To be sure, we therapists had been waiting a long, long time for a depiction of psychotherapy in the media that even approximates the complexity of real life we see in our offices. From *Dr. Dippy's Sanitarium* (1906) to *Hannibal* (2001), we have endured cinematic depictions of therapists that range from the buffoonish to the malevolent with very rare exceptions that approach what a therapist might actually do in practice. We've watched Peter Sellers attempt to seduce his women patients during group therapy in *What's New, Pussycat?* (1965). We've munched popcorn in darkened theaters while Woody Allen's other protagonists grow increasingly disillusioned with the therapeutic inaction of psychoanalysis. We've chuckled as Richard Dreyfuss unravels to the point of attempting to kill his patient (Bill Murray) in *What About Bob?* (1991). We've marveled as one beautiful female therapist after another succumbs to the charms of handsome male patients in movies like *Spellbound* (1945), *Knock on Wood* (1954), *Sex and the Single Girl* (1963), *The Man Who Loved Women* (1983) and *Prince of Tides* (1991). And, of course, our culinary preferences have been challenged by watching Hannibal Lecter sauté Ray Liotta's brains while making light conversation in the kitchen (although I think poor Hannibal is regarded with excessive harshness by my colleagues, especially since the American Psychiatric Association ethics code does not strictly forbid eating one's patients).

Television psychotherapists have not fared much better. They appear to be far more disturbed than their patients and seldom helpful to those who seek them out. I am aware that *Frasier* has been lavished with Emmy Awards and that Sidney Freedman helped Hawkeye work through a devastating trauma on *MASH*, but for the most part therapists on TV would not lead the average viewer to check the yellow pages for the nearest mental health clinic.

After a disconcerting history of more than four hundred American films featuring outrageous portrayals of mental health professionals at work, we psychotherapists have finally found a therapy process we can take seriously. Not only is the therapy an arguably accurate version of what actually happens in our consulting rooms, but the writers are blessed with an extraordinary psychological sophistication. The themes in Tony's life represented in the therapy are so complicated and compelling that they inspire collegial debate in the hallways of office buildings and at cocktail parties. Lorraine Bracco, who plays Dr. Melfi, and four of the show's five writers have been in psychotherapy themselves, and their experiences give the treatment an "inside" perspective that provides a ring of truth to the sessions between Tony and Dr. Melfi.

Not all mental health professionals are thrilled with the series or with the psychotherapy portrayed. The disagreements have prompted heated exchanges. In *Psychiatric News*, the official newspaper of the American Psychiatric Association, a reader asserted that he would flunk Dr. Melfi if he were examining her for the board certification exam because she colludes with her patient's antisocial behavior instead of confronting him about it. Another psychiatrist responded with an impassioned defense of Dr. Melfi: "I would dare say that *The Sopranos* has done more to destigmatize mental illness (through educating the public about such clinical diagnoses as panic disorder and antisocial and borderline personality disorders), reveal to the American public what goes on behind the closed doors of the therapist's office, and help define what a psychiatrist is than any public relations initiative ever promulgated by our own professional guild organization." He goes on to suggest that the American Psychiatric Association should honor the producers and writers. In fact, in December 2001, the American Psychoanalytic Association did present the producers and writers with an award for "the artistic depiction of psychoanalysis and psychoanalytic psychotherapy." Lorraine Bracco received an award at the same event for creating "the most credible psychoanalyst ever to appear in the cinema or on television."

Other colleagues criticize Dr. Melfi for telling Tony that if he reveals an intent to harm others, she will have to report him to the authorities. In their view, she has thus encouraged him to violate the fundamental rule of psychoanalytic therapy, which is to say whatever comes to mind without censoring. Still others have felt that Dr. Melfi is stiff and stilted in her style, heavy-handed, prone to speak in jargon and inclined toward lengthy psychoeducational monologues.

Because psychotherapists rarely see each other work with patients, however, there is no firm consensus about what constitutes a good session with a particular person. Hence, they may have dramatically different opinions on depictions of psychotherapy in a television series. One reason, though, that the psychotherapy in *The Sopranos* is so fascinating is that the writers make no attempt to idealize Dr. Melfi as an oracular source of truth. They have wisely chosen to show her as a professional and competent practitioner who is nevertheless troubled with conflicts of her own and with specific countertransference reactions to Tony. Countertransference—the therapist's emotional reactions to the patient—is an expectable part of any therapy process and a tool to help understand the therapeutic interaction. Dr. Melfi's mistakes and her own emotional struggles with Tony lend further credibility to the series—and are especially engaging to viewers on both sides of the couch.

The Sopranos also departs from the positive cinematic depiction of psychotherapists. In a brief golden age of psychotherapy and psychoanalysis in the cinema between 1957 and 1963, idealized portrayals of dramatic healing misrepresented psychotherapy as badly as the negative portrayals. Think of Simon Oakland's brilliant psychodynamic formulation of Norman Bates in *Psycho* (1960) or Lee J. Cobb's magnificent cure of Joanne Woodward in *The Three Faces of Eve* (1957). In the former, the psychiatrist explains all of Norman's psychopathology and even the location of the missing money after a couple of forensic interviews. In the latter, the therapist integrates the disparate aspects of his patient's multiple personality by hypnotizing her and encouraging her to recall a single traumatic memory from her childhood. With *The Sopranos*, it is refreshing to see a therapist who is neither devalued as contemptible and incompetent nor raised to a transcendent level of expertise.

Even though *The Sopranos* is about many other aspects of Tony Soprano's life, the psychotherapeutic relationship between Tony and Dr. Melfi is at its heart. Creator David Chase noted that the therapy session was the germ of his idea for the series. Everything grew from that central image. He has acknowledged in an interview that the sessions with Dr. Melfi reflect his own experience with the woman therapist he saw. He also said he was helped by three or four male therapists before he found her. He insisted on a high degree of realism: "It was very important to me to let the silences play that really happen in a psychiatrist's office."

To say that the therapy represented in *The Sopranos* is the most accurate and complex ever to appear on television or film is not the same as saying that it is identical to what transpires in the office of the typical female psychiatrist conducting psychoanalytic therapy with a Mafia don. It would be a challenge, of course, to find such a therapeutic pair anywhere in the entire psychoanalytic community. The notion that a powerful mobster would seek out twice-weekly analytic therapy with a gorgeous woman therapist is a conceit that tickles the funny bone of audiences, who find this high concept irresistible. At least producers think they do. *The Sopranos* series was the sixth time in the 1990s that a mobster visited a therapist to get in touch with his feelings. Bill Murray spouted psychobabble in the 1993 film *Mad Dog and Glory*. Four years later, John Cusack poured out his soul to psychiatrist Alan Arkin in *Grosse Pointe Blank*. The same year *National Lampoon's The Don's Analyst* appeared on cable with Robert Loggia as the don and Kevin Pollak as the analyst. In *Faithful* (1996), Chazz Palminteri makes phone calls to his therapist (played by the director, Paul Mazursky) while holding Cher hostage. And in *Analyze This* (1999) Robert DeNiro is a mobster who, like Tony, suffers from panic attacks and Billy Crystal is the therapist. (Coincidentally, their creators made *The Sopranos* and *Analyze This* without any knowledge of each other's projects.) There is something inherently reassuring in learning that hard-boiled criminals are really sensitive pussycats beneath the surface. All that mayhem, extortion and cruelty probably just stem from not being loved enough as children.

Media like television and film occupy a region between reality and illusion. This realm is known as a "play space," a concept derived from the work of the British analyst D.W. Winnicott. He refers to a psychological experience that begins between an infant and mother but arises later in other relationships. It is a psychological space between fantasy and reality and between one's inner and external worlds, and it plays a key role in the development of play, creativity and other factors that lend richness to human experience. In the ideal psychoanalytic treatment, the patient and analyst enter this space to explore aspects of the self that are based partly in fantasy and partly in reality. For example, you as a patient may experience your analyst "as if" he or she were your mother or father. This evocation of an old relationship may help you explore feelings toward the therapist that grow out of early experiences, and help you to see how you re-create these feelings in your present relationships.

The unlikely notion that a troubled mobster might visit a therapist for intensive psychoanalytic therapy is an example of entering this fantasy-saturated playground, though in reality such events are unlikely to unfold in just this way. However, if one accepts the premises of the treatment arrangement—if indeed a Mafia don were to actually enter treatment with a beautiful Italian-American psychiatrist, the therapy that unfolds in *The Sopranos* becomes compelling and believable.

The series' writers rarely miss an opportunity to have fun with the premise of a hard-boiled thug in a psychotherapist's office. When Tony decides to tell his henchmen that he has been seeing a psychiatrist, his colleagues react with stunned silence. Silvio Dante (Steven Van Zandt) finally breaks the silence with words of moral support: "I'm sure you did it with complete discretion." Paulie Walnuts (Tony Sirico) is similarly supportive, offering that "it's not the worst thing I ever heard." Then, swept up by the Oprah-like atmosphere in the room, Paulie goes further: "I was seeing a therapist myself about a year ago. I had some issues."

The use of a play space is not, of course, limited to the therapy scenes in *The Sopranos*. In one surreal episode, a huge Russian thug, a veteran from the war in Chechnya, is beaten, choked, thrown in a trunk and even shot in the head. Yet he won't die. Who is this guy? Tony calls Paulie on a cell phone that keeps breaking up during their conversation. He explains that the Russian killed sixteen Chechnyan rebels single-handed and was with the interior ministry. Paulie is duly impressed. Turning to Christopher, he says in awe, "He killed sixteen Czechoslovakians. The guy was an interior decorator." Christopher is unimpressed: "His house looked like shit," he retorts. Chase fully recognizes this departure from realism: "The Russian guy was like something out of a fairy tale. Well, not a fairy tale exactly. He's more like a spirit."

Audiences don't want to stare at the screen only to find themselves looking back. They seek out something larger than life, something of mythic proportions. Hence television and film have a mythopoetic function. The Mob has already been firmly entrenched in cultural mythology, so *The Sopranos* can build on *The Godfather, GoodFellas, Casino, Prizzi's Honor, The Untouchables* and numerous other Mafia films stored in viewers' memory banks. Chase is a great admirer of Martin Scorsese's *GoodFellas* (1990) and refers to it as "The Koran."

A recurrent theme in *The Sopranos* is the fluidity between life and art. When Christopher Moltisanti's (Michael Imperioli) friend Brendan is dispatched by a hit man with a bullet through the eye, Big Pussy Bompensiero (Vincent Pastore) comments that the hit was a "Moe Green special," referring to a similar killing in *The Godfather*. And throughout the series Silvio entertains his cronies with imitations of Al Pacino doing Michael Corleone. Paulie drives a car that plays *The Godfather* theme on its horn. Tony gets teary-eyed watching a video of Cagney in *The Public Enemy*.

There are homages to other films throughout *The Sopranos*. Christopher shoots a bakery clerk in the foot, recollecting a similar incident in *GoodFellas*, when Michael Imperioli played a waiter in a tavern who himself was shot in the foot by Joe Pesci's character. The bakery clerk screams, "You shot my foot!" As he walks out the door, Christopher says, "It happens"—a sly reference to his character in *GoodFellas*. Tony seeks out further therapy with a male therapist decked out in blue jeans, Western tie and cowboy boots. Tony uses a pseudonym to avoid recognition, but Dr. Hopalong is not fooled: "Mr. Spears . . . I watch the news like everyone else. I know who you are. And I saw *Analyze This*. I don't need the ramifications that could arise from treating someone like yourself." Tony pleads with him: "*Analyze This*? Come on, it's a fuckin' comedy!" The writers of *The Sopranos* know that life imitates art and vice versa, and they use this device with great flair.

In *The Sopranos*, art also imitates life. The nicknames "Big Pussy" and "Little Pussy" were taken from actual gangsters from the 1940s. Jerry Adler's character, Hesh, was based on a Jewish record producer in the 1950s who was reported to have had connections with the Gambino family. The blowing up of Artie's restaurant, Vesuvio's, paralleled a mob incident in Providence, Rhode Island. A hit was planned at the Providence establishment, so the restaurant was torched to avoid adverse publicity.

The writers are particularly fascinated with the role that film plays in how the mobsters form their identities. Christopher is a frustrated screenwriter, and the more he learns about screenwriting, the more he senses that his life falls short of the mobsters he sees in the movies. Over and over again he laments that while every character in the narrative of a film has "an arc," he himself has no arc.

During the second season, Christopher becomes obsessed with a film Jon Favreau is making on the streets of New Jersey and serves as a de facto consultant after he shows up on the set and advises the director on the proper use of indigenous slang for female genitalia. Favreau and his assistant Amy (Alicia Witt) listen intently to Christopher as he tells about a colleague of his who was getting a blow job from a gorgeous woman, only to discover the "she" is a "he." Amy chimes in: "*Crying Game.*" Favreau corrects her sternly: "It's a true story." Although life is like a film in some ways, it's not the same thing. Christopher's stint as technical advisor is less than auspicious, however, and he returns to his humdrum existence as a foot soldier in Tony Soprano's army.

In one of the more amusing scenes, we see Dr. Melfi at home with her parents and her son, Jason. For reasons that are not clear, her ex-husband is also present at the dinner table.

She has let slip that she is treating a Mafia don, and her ex-husband gets on his soapbox about the stigma attached to being Italian American. He tells her that five thousand Mafia members give a bad name to twenty million Italian Americans. To his surprise, his son Jason jumps to the defense of the stereotype, pointing out that Italian mobster movies are classic American cinema like Westerns, giving iconic and mythic status to Italian gangsters. Jennifer's father agrees with his grandson.

The art-imitating-life-imitating-art dimension of *The Sopranos* seemed particularly uncanny in July 2001, when 16-year-old Robert Iler, who plays Tony's son, A.J., was arrested in Manhattan for robbing two teens on the Upper East Side of about $40. *Sopranos* fans reacted with a mixture of fascination and disbelief. Iler is not the first actor on the show whose real life matched his screen identity. Tony Sirico, who plays Paulie Walnuts, was arrested twenty-eight times and sent to jail twice for a total of seven years before he became an actor. He was almost a made man in the Mob but stopped himself from taking that final step. He still has a scar where a bullet entered his leg.

Not surprisingly, real-life organized crime figures have become regular viewers of *The Sopranos*. Writing in the *New Yorker*, David Remnick reports on a wiretapped conversation between mobsters recorded on March 3, 1999. A capo named Anthony Rotondo and an enforcer named Joseph Sclafani commented on the similarities between local mobsters and

Tony's gang. They offered positive critiques of the acting and writing, but Sclafani clearly felt slighted by the lack of attention to him in the episodes. "I'm not even existing over there," he concluded.

The writers' pitch-perfect understanding of their characters' inner world is beautifully displayed in their portrayal of Christopher. Like Sclafani, he feels unrecognized. When he watches a TV news exposé of the Soprano family, he worries only that his name is not mentioned. He is devastated when his colleagues are named and he isn't. In one reflective moment, he laments, "The fuckin' regularness of life is too fuckin' hard for me." His source of suffering is a sense of existential meaninglessness, a feeling of being doomed to an unobserved life where he is a pawn in a chess game beyond his comprehension. He regards his very being as an inconsequential nothingness. When Christopher's name finally does appear in the news, he is ecstatic and speeds to the corner newspaper dispenser, where he removes the entire stack of newspapers to be sure all his friends and relatives are informed that he is no longer a nobody.

This theme of being a nobody runs through *The Sopranos*. Matthew Bevilaqua (Lillo Brancato, Jr.) and Sean Gismonte (Chris Tardio) are two young goons who work for Christopher at his scam stockbroker operation. Like *Hamlet*'s Rosencrantz and Guildenstern, they feel cut off from the action—mere observers of the movers and shakers who shape the events around them. They eagerly inquire of Christopher, "Does Tony ever talk about us?" The answer is a deadpan "No." The solution to their existential angst is one with overtones of Camus's *The Stranger*—they will establish a sense of authenticity and identity through the act of murder. They pay for it, of course, with their lives. A variation on this theme is repeated when Jackie Aprile, Jr., (Jason Cerbone) and his cronies decide to transcend their status as losers by robbing a group of made men at a poker game. The same consequence awaits them. In *Being and Nothingness*, his effort to banish the dualism of being and appearance, Sartre declared: "The act is everything."

The most striking example of this quest for heroic status occurs in the moving episode when the aging mobster Bobby Bacala, Sr. (Burt Young) strives to be "useful" as he is succumbing to lung cancer. He jumps at the opportunity to bump off his godson as a way of going out in a blaze of glory. Only through extraordinary persistence is he able to pull off his assignment, and he is elated as he drives away from the crime scene. His celebration is interrupted, however, when he dies at the wheel. The viewer, like Bacala himself, derives some satisfaction that he has died with his boots on.

Death hangs heavy over *The Sopranos*. Funerals are a regular feature. When it's not a hit man (or constipated bowels), it's cancer. In the same episode in which time runs out for old man Bacala, Uncle Junior (Dominic Chianese) is diagnosed with colon cancer. In a moment of profound empathy, Tony's sister Janice (Aida Turturro) comments, "Another toothpick," a term she learned from her equally empathic mother, Livia, to describe the wasted appearance of the cancer victims in the family.

Ernest Becker, in his 1973 Pulitzer Prize–winning book *The Denial of Death*, said that the problem of heroics is the central dilemma of life. Facing the certainty of death, how does one achieve a measure of immortality in an otherwise humdrum life? He describes human heroics as "a blind driven-ness that burns people up; in passionate people, a screaming for glory as uncritical and reflexive as the howling of a dog." The howling is especially shrill in *The Sopranos*, where being a grunt in the Mafia hierarchy is a dreaded fate.

Death is the great leveler. Every viewer glued to the television set on Sunday evenings knows that death is the ultimate certainty. We all want to make an impact, leave a trace of some kind. We, too, feel like grunts in the game of life. We, too, know that we could be snuffed out tomorrow by a terrorist attack, a coronary or a drunk driver. When we watch Tony and his gang, we see ourselves racing against time to make a mark before the final curtain.

With life imitating art so intensely, it is not surprising that the cast of *The Sopranos* worries a good deal about whom Chase will whack next. Death in *The Sopranos* means loss of a regular job. At one point Gandolfini was so worried about getting killed off that he called Chase at home to ask him if his character was in danger.

Even Tony's son, A.J., sounds like a nihilist. When his grandmother Livia (Nancy Marchand) tells him about a group of teenagers killed when their overcrowded car hit a tree, he comments: "Those kids, they're dead meat. What's the use? What's the purpose?" Livia makes no attempt to revise his thinking. She advises him not to expect happiness and succinctly summarizes her view of life: "It's all a big nothing."

These concerns about death, meaning, being and nothingness pervade the series, and Tony himself struggles with them in psychotherapy. Indeed, the fact that Tony is in psychotherapy allows viewers to penetrate his interior world, which would be otherwise unavailable to us. Psychotherapy often serves as a plot device in film. A novel's narrator can inform the reader about the protagonist's inner struggles, but a film has no such omniscient observer. One solution is to have the central character in a film visit a psychotherapist to reveal an inner monologue. In *The Hospital* (1971), written by Paddy Chayefsky, the audience finds out that the character played by George C. Scott is seriously suicidal when he stops in to chat with a psychiatrist colleague. In *Klute* (1971), Jane Fonda's high-priced prostitute talks to a psychotherapist about her internal struggles showing that she is more complicated than her call girl activities suggest.

Tony's psychotherapy with Dr. Melfi serves a similar purpose. The history taking of a first psychotherapy session conveniently paints a picture of Tony's life. Flashbacks illustrate what Tony is telling Dr. Melfi about his symptoms, his family and his background. The writers use this exposition technique to comic effect, juxtaposing the sanitized version of events that Tony reports to Dr. Melfi with flashbacks of the violent altercations that actually took place.

The comparisons between psychotherapy in film and in *The Sopranos* are instructive, but limited. One cannot capture the complexity of a psychoanalytic psychotherapy process in a two-hour feature film. One of the reasons the therapy in *The Sopranos* is so convincing is that over thirty-nine episodes in three years of viewing, the writers can illustrate the slings and arrows of outrageous transference, countertransference and acting out.

One reason *The Sopranos* is so satisfying is that it conveys life in all its complexity. The therapy scenes contribute to that complexity, because the coin of the realm in psychoanalytic therapy is multiple determination, where a symptom's multi-layered meanings unfold gradually as one layer is peeled off to reveal another. Consider the fear of speaking in public, a common phobia that brings many people to therapy. On the surface, it may seem to come from a dread of being exposed or of failing. But upon closer examination, therapist and patient often discover that fear of success, not failure, is actually driving the anxiety.

Nothing conveys complexity quite as directly as therapy, and therapy abounds in *The Sopranos*. Besides her sessions with Tony, Dr. Melfi goes to her own psychotherapist, Elliot Kupferberg, played by film director Peter Bogdanovich. Carmela has a confrontational consultation with one of Dr. Melfi's teachers, and she also attends sessions with Tony in Dr.

Melfi's office. In the first season, a clinical psychologist evaluates A.J. for attention deficit disorder after he gets into trouble at school. In an improbable but amusing scene, Dr. Melfi, her son and her ex-husband appear in the office of a family therapist (Sam Coppola) to discuss what she should do about seeing a mob kingpin in therapy.

At its core, *The Sopranos* is a tragicomedy exploring American values and the moral ambiguity of our age. In the same way that Quentin Tarantino loves to depict sleazeballs struggling with moral dilemmas in such films as *Pulp Fiction* (1994), Chase has fun with the clash between God, mother and apple pie, on the one hand, and money, sex and corruption, on the other. Like Samuel Beckett's tramps in *Waiting for Godot*, Chase's characters entertain us by wringing humor and meaning out of the fabric of a bleak backdrop of nothingness. Even though *The Sopranos* is entertainment, it teaches us something about ourselves that warrants a closer look. As Nancy Franklin noted in her *New Yorker* review, *The Sopranos*, in contrast to *Analyze This*, "gives you something—almost too many things—to think about." And as Gandolfini commented in an interview, "I have learned a hell of a lot from this show . . . just from the sessions with Dr. Melfi alone, about human beings. David Chase has taught me a great deal about depression and about anger and about things that I never knew about. And you come home, and you think about them."

In addition to providing complexity, the writers have produced a play space that appeals to all sorts of viewers. The music used in the series ranges from Sinatra to grand opera to rap, a diversity emblematic of the varied audience the show reaches. The power of the narrative, the characters and the psychological themes transcends television conventions, political correctness and viewer expectation.

The ubiquity of psychotherapy in *The Sopranos* offers a sophisticated rendering of fundamental human dilemmas rarely portrayed in any medium. Many therapists have reported increases in male patients as a result of *The Sopranos*. One can speculate that the windows on the unconscious mind that psychoanalytic approaches open up in the series may suggest a renewal of interest in the in-depth exploration of the individual psyche. Although the time-intensive techniques of this kind of treatment run against the grain of today's more fashionable pill-popping, we still have a hunger to know ourselves. Critic Ellen Willis points out, "Our culture's flight from psychoanalysis is not permanent." The pendulum is swinging back, and the motion of that pendulum may have been influenced by a cable series about the relationship between a mobster and a therapist.

TONY'S AILMENT:
JANUS IN JERSEY

Tony's psychiatric diagnosis has stirred intense controversy among mental health professionals who watch *The Sopranos*. Is he a psychopath who is essentially untreatable? Is Dr. Melfi wasting her time? Can he be a true psychopath and still have such loving feelings for his family? Is he anxious or depressed? Does he have true panic disorder or syncopal (fainting) episodes? Is his personality best described as borderline, narcissistic or antisocial?

Even Tony's wife, Carmela (played by Edie Falco), is puzzled by her husband's clinical picture. In one episode she asks a smug Tony why he is smiling. When he is silent and mysterious in response, she narrows her diagnosis to three possibilities: "I can't tell if you're just old-fashioned, paranoid or a fuckin' asshole."

From a psychiatric perspective, Tony's ailment is anything but straightforward. His ticket of admission to Dr. Melfi's office is the panic attack that led him to consult with his internist neighbor. Dr. Cusemano (Robert Lupone) suggests three psychiatrists, two of them Jewish males, and the third, Dr. Jennifer Melfi. Tony picks Dr. Melfi because he assumes that she is Italian American. He explains to Dr. Melfi during their first session that the panic attacks started when the ducks visiting his swimming pool flew away. Panic attacks are discrete periods of intense discomfort or fear, often escalating to a sense of impending doom; they generally last only a few minutes. Common symptoms include palpitations, shakiness, shortness of breath, chest pain, nausea, sweating, dizziness or lightheadedness, fear of dying, fear of losing control or going crazy and sometimes tingling sensations. Imagine for a moment that you are on an elevator when the power suddenly goes out. The lights flicker and die. The elevator abruptly stops. You find it hard to breathe. You start perspiring. You wonder if you'll ever be found. You suddenly panic and reach for the phone. There is no dial tone. This scenario approximates the terror of a panic attack. Tony's case is unusual because he actually faints and loses consciousness. More typically, the person fears he will pass out but never actually loses consciousness. Tony's fainting, though, is an effective dramatic touch. Art prevailed over science.

This symptomatic picture was not chosen at random. David Chase stressed, "It was important that he have a physical manifestation caused by psychological things because I believe a tough-guy gangster wouldn't go in and say, 'I'm depressed.' It wouldn't work. But if he had a physical disability, it would be believable. It would be okay."

In the course of the first session, though, Tony also tells his psychiatrist that he has been depressed ever since the ducks left his pool. Before long, Tony is clearly depressed to the point where he's staying in bed all the time. Carmela worries and suggests that "the lady shrink" needs to give him more medication. Since he appears to be taking both Prozac and lithium by the handful, rather than how they're actually prescribed, we cannot be certain if his apparent depression is partly toxicity from the lithium or a condition independent of the medication. In the midst of his toxic delirium, he hallucinates a beautiful Italian woman nursing her baby as he looks on.

In that same episode Tony tells Dr. Melfi that he feels dead and empty, and she is so concerned about his potential for suicide that she even suggests a residential treatment center. Tony declines her offer, of course, but she increases his Prozac to 60 mg a day. By the end of the episode, she has taken him off lithium, which was used to "kick start" the Prozac. He appears much less depressed at the end of the episode, but he has also been energized by the adrenalin rush associated with his escape from a botched hit by two contract killers.

Tony Soprano has the good fortune to be referred to a psychoanalytically trained psychiatrist, who knows that the symptomatic tip of the iceberg may herald the presence of deeper layers of conflict and suffering that are not immediately apparent. Dr. Melfi recognizes that the anxiety Tony reports is a signal of profound distress. She also knows that the origins of that distress are largely outside Tony's conscious awareness. A psychoanalytic therapist would assume that her patient's defenses were failing for some reason and that the anxiety was a flare sent up from his unconscious.

Although panic attacks may appear to have no psychological content, there are often identifiable triggers. And this is the case with Tony. He has his first attack when the birds fly away and leave him alone. Threats involving the potential loss of a much-loved person are particularly likely to trigger panic. Tony suffers a second panic attack after he has put his mother into a retirement home and is taking her picture off the mantle in her house.

A middle-aged Mafia boss is suddenly afraid of being left alone. He moves his mother out of her home and into an anteroom to eternity. He is losing control of his children, who are increasingly defiant, and he is worried about his marriage. Tony's condition is not limited to a panicky feeling that he will lose someone important to him. He is also depressed. Anxiety and depression are related, and it is common for patients to experience both conditions. They have similar chemical abnormalities in the brain, and they respond to the same medications. We think of anxiety as the anticipation of a terrible event that may occur in the future, whereas depression is the conviction that a catastrophe has already happened. We may be anxious about a hijacking when we board a plane, but we feel sadness and grief about those who perished in the hijackings on September 11, 2001. Loss is often the theme of both anxiety and depression. Such is the case with Tony.

Anxiety and depression are syndromes or symptomatic disorders as opposed to disorders of *personality*. Many psychiatrists feel this distinction is merely Jesuitical hairsplitting, but clinicians typically think about the patient's character as separate from the symptoms the patient is complaining about, and many choose to ignore personality traits or character altogether while aggressively treating the symptoms with medication.

Jennifer Melfi, however, is a psychoanalyst (we frequently see the analyst's couch strategically placed in one corner of her office), and she rushes in where all too many biological psychiatrists fear to tread. Even in the first session, knowing of his notoriety, she asks Tony if he's comfortable with the way he makes his living. In other words, she challenges his very essence because she senses that his symptoms of anxiety and depression cannot be entirely divorced from who he is. Personality is the soil from which symptoms emerge.

This consideration of Tony Soprano's underlying character structure brings us to a controversy that has hovered over the series since its inception: Is Tony a psychopath? Critic Nancy Franklin wonders, "Is there a point to understanding that someone who's a lifelong criminal and brutal killer is not *just* a brutal killer? This conundrum is somehow embedded in every moment of the show." Is he a cruel, remorseless, ruthless, sadistic, exploitative, womanizing, thoroughly corrupt sleazoid personality disorder? Or is he simply an all-American Everyman, the prototypical struggling businessman who bends the rules to get ahead but nevertheless loves his family and tries to do what is best for them?

The term "psychopath" is not part of psychiatry's official diagnostic manual. It was originally used to describe people who totally disregard the law and are completely unable to empathize with the feelings or concerns of others. In the latter half of the twentieth century, the term "psychopath" fell out of favor. "Antisocial personality disorder" became the preferred diagnostic label for corrupt people who had no regard for the laws of civilization. This terminology has been widely criticized, however, because it casts too broad a net.

Because of these criticisms, the term "psychopath" is currently making a comeback. It now refers to a person prone to criminal behavior who has a sadomasochistic style of interacting with others based on power and a total absence of remorse for the harm he does. In fact, a psychopath enjoys the suffering he inflicts. He is not capable of loyalty and loving emotional attachments. The psychopath can look you in the eye, tell you his last dollar was blown away in a hurricane and charm you into giving him $5,000 on the spot. I once evaluated a man who read the obituaries to identify grieving widows who would be easy prey for him. He would take them into his confidence, use their credit cards, deplete their bank accounts and disappear when the money was gone.

Psychopathy accounts for many of the hard-boiled criminals who are in and out of the prison system throughout their lives, but these con men are only a minority of the total prison population. In one study 75 percent of prison inmates met the official diagnostic criteria for antisocial personality disorder, but only 25 percent of the total inmate population were diagnosable as psychopaths. Not all criminals are in prison, however. Some are politicians, doctors, lawyers—even psychotherapists.

A good deal of research has gone into the causes of antisocial behavior. Much of this research makes no distinction between the antisocial personality disorder and psychopathy. Nevertheless, there are clear patterns. Some combination of genes and environment appears to be at work. In studies of twins in which the relative influence of inherited traits and environmental adversity can be teased out, both nature and nurture appear to be important. Childhood neglect and abuse also appear to play a role in the development of antisocial symptoms.

Since the revival of interest in psychopathy as a narrower category, research has begun to document that psychopaths differ dramatically from other people in the way they react to situations. In the face of danger, they show none of the signs of fear or anxiety that the rest of us manifest. Recall Hannibal

Lecter's attack on an electrocardiogram technician discussed in Thomas Harris's *Red Dragon* about the fictional psychopath. While Hannibal the Cannibal was viciously biting off the poor technician's tongue, his EKG recording showed no variation in his pulse.

These physiological observations suggest that they are not particularly distressed by lying, cheating, stealing or killing. Only their own needs matter to them. They are profoundly detached from all human relationships and from emotional experience in general. They cannot learn values from their parents in the way that most of us do, so their behavior is not subject to pangs of conscience. A psychopath would not do well in Tony Soprano's Mob family. Loyalty to others and a deep bond of attachment are absolutely necessary to survive in that family. The true psychopath, such as Harold Konigsberg, whose checkered career was recently featured in the *New Yorker*, might be peripherally involved with organized crime but not generally linked with one family. Konigsberg, in fact, was hired as a hit man by a variety of different Mob families. He killed coldly and ruthlessly and took particular pleasure in showing that he was smarter than judges and attorneys.

When psychopaths do find their way into Mob families, they are regarded as troublemakers who disrupt business operations. In *The Sopranos*, Richie Aprile (David Proval) and Ralph Ciforetto (Joe Pantoliano) are probably psychopaths. Both are scheming and ruthless manipulators. Neither shows the slightest loyalty in the way they move within the Mob. They are so self-absorbed they remind us of one definition of narcissism—a person who shouts his own name during orgasm. In Martin Scorsese's *GoodFellas*, the unforgettable character played by Joe Pesci is a quintessential psychopath, creating major problems for his fellow gangsters by shooting people for sport and otherwise indulging in reptilian pleasures.

Psychopaths abound in the cinema. Because they are the embodiment of pure evil, they serve as marvelous foils for the hero, who can feel entirely justified in rubbing them out. In the 1990 film *Internal Affairs*, Richard Gere plays a crooked cop named Dennis Peck who kills with impunity and manipulates everyone in the police force to his own advantage through extortion schemes. Ben Kingsley's character in *Sexy Beast* (2001), a five-star psychopath if there ever was one, is so nasty that Gandhi himself would blow him away. Kevin Spacey's performances in *Se7en* (1995) and *The Usual Suspects* (1995) as, respectively, a deranged killer and a deranged killer are other chilling examples of psychopathy on the silver screen.

Our current understanding of psychopathy leads us to an unequivocal conclusion: Tony Soprano may not be New Jersey's version of Mother Teresa, but he is clearly not a true psychopath. He has profound and loving relationships in both his families—Carmela and his children at home and the gang down at the Bada Bing. Despite his philandering, he loves Carmela and is intensely loyal to her in his own way. And Tony is far from a man without conscience. When he is tipped off that Big Pussy may be wired, he is deeply troubled that his friend could betray him and comments, "I don't like him—I love him." Before he can authorize a hit on Big Pussy, he tells Paulie that he must be "110 percent sure." When Dr. Melfi cautions him that harboring secrets can lead to mind-burdening guilt, Tony listens intently to her.

The three seasons of *The Sopranos* provide abundant evidence that Tony is capable of genuine concern. After Dr. Melfi's rape, he is visibly distressed at her condition and expresses sincere interest in helping her. He takes a fatherly role with Tracee (Ariel Kelly), the Bada Bing dancer and prostitute who is ultimately beaten to death by Ralphie. He tells her to avoid Ralphie and save her body for dancing. When she makes overtures to him, he rejects her offers and informs her that he has a family.

Tony Soprano lives by a moral code. True, his moral compass does not lead him in the direction of society's laws, but in his world, loyalty is rewarded, and disloyalty is punished. Those who get whacked deserve it because they have betrayed him. Tony does not take sadistic pleasure in the suffering of others. He is more interested in maintaining order and discipline through a combination of respect and fear. He sees random violence as a reflection of weakness and poor judgment.

Yet there is no question that Tony is a thug. He rules the Mob by brute force. He kills if necessary. He lies when he needs to. He steals from others. He treats his goomahs (girl-friends) with contempt. Indeed, his concern for Tracee doesn't prevent him from using and discarding a series of other pros-titutes. David Chase puts it concisely. Defending the show's violence, he says with characteristic understatement: "These are not nice people, for the most part."

Tony's dual nature is best depicted in the much discussed episode when he takes his daughter, Meadow (Jamie-Lynn Sigler), on a trip through New England to look at colleges. She confronts him with his Mob connections and tells him that sometimes she wishes he were like other dads. Over a can-dlelit dinner, Tony tells Meadow how proud he is of her and explains that there was a time when Italians did not have many choices. Ever the skeptic, Meadow retorts, "Yeah, like Mario Cuomo?" In the same conversation she confesses that she has taken speed, and Tony at first threatens to slap her but then calms down and listens. Meadow says she's glad they have the kind of relationship in which she can be honest with him. In the midst of this idyllic father–daughter bonding, Tony spots a rat who turned government witness and is now in hid-ing as a travel agent. Tony is seething with revenge because the rat's testimony resulted in the murder of a close associate. He tracks him down and garrotes him, pausing to watch Canadian geese flying in formation before he leaves the murder scene.

David Chase reports that HBO originally objected to this scene where Tony kills the Judas with his bare hands. They argued that he had built up the most interesting protagonist in twenty-five years of television, and they worried that this scene would cause audiences to lose sympathy for Tony. Chase argued exactly the opposite: If Tony did not kill the rat, his character would lose credibility and the series would lose viewers. Chase prevailed.

To pursue his nemesis, Tony disappears suddenly at several points during the college visits, and Meadow begins to question him. He lies to cover his tracks, and Meadow is skeptical: "You're being honest with me, aren't you? We have that kind of relationship." He lies again, and Meadow is clearly disappointed but says, "I love you," and Tony responds in kind.

Near the end of this episode, Tony is sitting in a hallway in the Bowdoin College admissions building. He looks up and reads a quote from one of their illustrious graduates, Nathaniel Hawthorne: "No man can wear one face to himself and another to the multitude without finally getting bewildered as to which may be true." The two sides of Tony are so clearly juxtaposed in his New England college tour that even he cannot deny the disparity between the different sectors of his personality. Like the mythical solar deity Janus, who had one face for the rising sun and another for the sunset, Tony wears two faces.

This Janus-like dimension is pivotal. Chase observed that Tony's character actually crystallized for him when he realized that he could turn on a dime from humane concern and affection to frightening rage toward those he loved. He cites a scene in which Christopher toys with the idea of leaving the

Mob and going to Hollywood. Tony becomes enraged and grabs Christopher by the lapels with his full fury. In seconds he is once again tender to his surrogate son and clearly proud to be associated with him.

Kindness and anger coexist in Tony. Some of our most successful and charismatic leaders have that same propensity to shift abruptly from generosity and support to seething rage. Think of the football coach who praises his athletes and treats them like his own children and then berates them when they do not give him one hundred percent effort on the playing field. The audience's continued involvement with Tony and his merry band of thieves demands that they see a soft and vulnerable side. A cold-blooded psychopath would be unlikely to hold an audience's rapt attention for thirty-nine episodes. The series succeeds because Tony is human. He suffers like the rest of us. At the end of the third season, he tearfully asks Dr. Melfi, "Why does everything gotta be so hard? I'm not saying I'm perfect. But I do the right thing by my family. Doesn't that count for anything?" Indeed.

The creative staff of *The Sopranos*—producers, directors, writers and actors—are careful to maintain the viewers' sympathy with Tony. Gandolfini analyzed why the audience likes Tony: ". . . people watch Tony, and they watch his mother giving him shit and his wife giving him shit. Even his girlfriend throws shit at him, you know. So here's this powerful figure getting abused all the time." When Ralphie becomes the bête noire of the family by bashing Tracee's brains in, Tony is the white knight who has the guts to strike a made man for his senseless violence. By clever crosscutting between Tracee and Meadow, the show highlights Tony's compassion.

As the strategically placed Hawthorne quote suggests, Tony Soprano is split down the middle. Some critics have suggested that it is out of character for him to be a loving family man at the same time he is a vicious criminal, but, in fact, as a person with serious personality disorders, he is most "in character" when he appears to be "out of character." Hence the depiction of Tony as a complex mixture of a loving paterfamilias and a ruthless criminal actually lends credibility to the series. Joe Pistone, who spent six years in deep cover as Donnie Brasco and lived among Mob families, confirms this credibility. He has vouched for the authenticity of Tony's portrayal and has stressed that Chase's details are on the money.

The concept of "splitting," first described by Freud, explains how a person can harbor contradictory attitudes, beliefs and behaviors, keeping them safely separate from one another with a healthy dose of denial. The separation is not as extreme as the division in multiple personality disorder (now called *dissociative identity disorder*), because the disparate halves are consciously aware of each other. (By contrast, the primary "personality" in true dissociative identity disorder is generally not aware of the other "personalities.") The term "vertical split" has been coined to describe this type of defense. The result is that the person is not terribly conflicted by the incompatibility of different sectors of the personality.

When others point out the contradictions, he may react with bland indifference—"What's the big deal?" In fact, the reason for the defensive splitting is to keep these contradictory parts unintegrated so they do not create conflict, anxiety and psychic pain.

A striking example of splitting occurred in a personality-disordered priest who was accused of having sex with adolescent boys and girls. In the psychiatric hospital it was pointed out that the priest tested positive for syphilis. The priest's response was, "That's impossible. I'm a celibate priest." The doctor, puzzled by his patient's answer, asked, "But I thought you were here because you were having sex with adolescent boys and girls. Isn't that correct?" The priest responded, "Well, I'm human." Here we see an example of two "selves," a "pedophile priest" and a "celibate priest," existing side by side and creating concern—if not utter confusion—in others because of their inherent contradiction. The priest, on the other hand, wonders why anyone would react so strongly, comfortably dismissing the contradiction with a patently preposterous explanation.

Even though the denial of the contradiction is conscious, it is not "chosen." Keeping the impulsive or violent behavior disconnected is an automatic response that helps preserve a stable sense of integrity. Silvio and Tony can thus talk about blowing up Artie's restaurant while cheering Meadow at her volleyball game. Paulie and Christopher pursue Mikey through the woods with intent to whack while simultaneously worrying about getting poison ivy. This alternation between the ordinary and the extraordinary is at the very core of *The Sopranos*.

Tony's effort to maintain the disavowal is repeatedly challenged in his relationships with his wife and children. Even though Meadow and A.J. have read about Tony's Mafia connection on the Internet, Tony tries to maintain the conceit that he is in waste management. When Junior's arrest is on the evening news, Tony is exasperated and tells Meadow that Junior is a legitimate businessman. Meadow responds with her laser-beam candor: "Cut the crap." She turns to A.J. and says, "Uncle Junior got busted." A.J. says, "Cool!" Tony, who does not like his denial punctured so bluntly, slaps A.J. on the head. Tony's children will not collude with him. Tony, on the other hand, has actually started to believe that he and Junior are legitimate businessmen and is taken aback by his children's rudeness. Both humor and pathos emerge from this premise.

In his study of how Nazi doctors could work at Auschwitz, Robert Jay Lifton coined the term "doubling" to characterize how the self was divided into two functioning wholes. By maintaining this double self, the Nazi doctors could forsake their fundamental oath to cure disease. They could spend their days committing genocide and their evenings listening to Mozart and helping their children with their homework. Lifton notes that extreme conditions in certain subcultures make this type of doubling almost a necessity to adapt and survive. He particularly cites the Mafia and Central American "death squads." Doubling enables one to tap into the evil inherent in all of us while maintaining a myth that one is not evil.

Lifton later studied fanatical religious cults and found similar mechanisms at work. In his investigation of the Aum Shinrikyo, a Japanese cult that released deadly nerve gas on subway trains in 1995 in Tokyo during rush hour, he examined both the cult leader and the followers. The leader, Shoko Asahara, led his group to justify apocalyptic violence in the name of religious principles. Lifton observed that cult leaders often have the same form of division within the self. Charismatic gurus may have the capacity for loving attachment and altruism in one corner of the psyche while promoting violence and mayhem from another sector. Because the disparate aspects of the self remain unintegrated, they are less prone to come into conflict with one another and therefore less likely to cause guilt. Hence the cult leader, or the Mob boss, may present an absolute certainty and conviction that is enormously appealing to lost souls who gravitate toward cults or Mob families.

This doubling, or vertical split, in the personality is a universal tendency. In certain circumstances, such as the horrors of combat, it is an adaptive form of psychological survival. If a soldier can convince himself that the enemy is the embodiment of evil, he can then maintain the perspective that murder is in the service of an altruistic and worthy cause. As Lifton puts it, "We have the paradox of a 'killing self' being created on behalf of what one perceives as one's own healing or survival."

In a similar vein, the terrorists who hijacked passenger jets and crashed them into the World Trade Center cannot be dismissed simply as "crazies." They studied in flight schools, frequented Daytona Beach strip clubs and passed for assimilated immigrants within the borders of the United States. While appearing to endorse American values, they were ecstatic at the prospect of taking their own lives and thousands of other lives with them in the pursuit of a religious cause. The "killing self" can also be created on behalf of a transcendent cause.

Eleven million viewers tune in to *The Sopranos* for all sorts of reasons, including great acting, clever dialogue, gruesome violence, nude women and scenic views of New Jersey. But one thing unites us: We will lose interest if we don't see the protagonist as someone with whom we can identify and sympathize. We recognize that we are all a mosaic of sorts. All of our parts don't necessarily gel into a coherent whole. Haven't we all committed acts that are morally dubious? And don't we all try to push those memories to the farthest corners of our consciousness? James Gandolfini noted in an interview: "I heard David Chase say one time that it's about people who lie to themselves, as we all do. Lying to ourselves on a daily basis and the mess it creates." Splitting is a method of avoiding internal conflict, especially moral conflict about the consequences of our behavior.

Indeed, concern about our own moral transgressions draws us to spend Sunday evenings watching Tony struggling with his complicated conscience. Americans have always been fascinated by the con artist who can get away with things that the rest of can't. As long ago as 1857, in his novel *The Confidence Man*, Herman Melville explored with considerable perceptiveness the dynamics between the con artist and those who are conned. The outlaw hero is a familiar part of American cinematic mythology. We laugh when Paul Newman and Robert Redford triumph in *The Sting*. Many of us secretly admire the smooth-talking, antisocial person who manages to write his own laws and follow his own moral code. Even psychotherapists cheer for McMurphy (Jack Nicholson) in *One Flew Over the Cuckoo's Nest*, an antisocial personality if there ever was one, when he nearly destroys the hospital's treatment program and gives Nurse Ratched her comeuppance. In the 1970s, D. B. Cooper became a folk hero when he robbed a bank, hijacked a plane and bailed out over the Pacific Northwest never to be seen again. A hit song assured his immortality, and T-shirts bearing his name were seen everywhere.

Another element pulls us into Tony Soprano's orbit. When we see his love for his family and his fatherly devotion to Christopher and Jackie, Jr., we experience a tantalizing hint of the potential for change. Maybe a bad man can become a good man. Maybe psychotherapy will transform him. Perhaps the caring attention of a devoted woman like Jennifer Melfi will repair the damage done by Livia. This need to believe in potential goodness is exactly what happens to therapists who treat antisocial personality disorders. Like Jennifer Melfi, we don't want to accept that Tony is a lost cause. We collude with the vertical split by ignoring the bad and focusing on the good.

Who we are is forged in the crucible of relatedness. Hence, divisions within us have corresponding divisions within our perceptions of others. The scene that crystallized Tony's dual nature for Chase typifies this inextricable link between self and other. Christopher is the loyal foot soldier for whom Tony is mentor, father figure and role model. Tony, in turn, regards him with fatherly pride. But when Christopher, disenchanted with his lowly position in the tribe, begins to dream of Hollywood, Tony becomes enraged and his view of Christopher changes dramatically. The loyal disciple has been transformed into a traitor.

His "vertical split" helps Tony preserve his self-respect, but maintaining the division takes its toll. The illusion that the separateness can avoid guilt and conflict requires an extraordinary degree of self-deception, which Tony—or anyone else in that kind of position—is unlikely to be able to sustain over a lifetime. The wall between Tony Soprano's two lives has begun to crumble when he first seeks out psychiatric treatment. His defenses are not as effective as they once were. His children know he's in the Mafia. Carmela knows he is a philanderer. He knows he is a fraud.

Tony has reached his peak in the twilight of the godfathers. Television news constantly reminds him that the spine of the Mob has been broken. Mobsters who are nailed by the FBI turn government witness and wear a wire that will betray their entire "family." The moral character of the mob has flown away like the ducks in Tony's swimming pool. At one point, Tony slumps at the foot of his bed while Carmela comforts him, and he wonders aloud, "What kind of person can I be that my own mother wants me dead? . . . My self-esteem is nonexistent right now. When I see my boys, all I feel is humiliation."

Tony relates a dream to Dr. Melfi in his very first session. In the dream his belly button is a Phillips head screw. When he unscrews it, his penis falls off. Tony picks it up and is looking for someone to put it back on when a bird flies down and plucks it out of his hand. As he talks about the dream, he breaks down and cries. He remembers how sad he was to see the ducks leave and says that when they gave birth to the baby ducks, it was like a family. In the midst of his tears he says he doesn't know what he's afraid of.

The audience is not sure what Tony is afraid of, either. The dream, which was based on a real dream that one of the directors shared with David Chase, is more than a straightforward depiction of castration anxiety. The bird swooping down and plucking the penis out of his hand and his sobbing as he contemplates the loss of the duck family suggest something far more complex.

He is afraid of loss, but the writers leave the exact nature of that loss a mystery. Is it the loss of his stature as head of the family? His anticipated decline, aging and deterioration? Loss of his mother? Of his sense of himself as a man? Of his children as they leave the nest?

One thing is clear: Tony has lost a certain view of the way the world should be and particularly his role in that world. He can't resurrect the post–World War II era, when men were men, women were women and the Mob had respect. He laments to Dr. Melfi that he has ended up in therapy. He says that Gary Cooper wasn't in touch with his feelings; he just did what he had to do. The plot on his life engineered by his mother and his uncle is the last straw. Accepting this undeniable conclusion makes Tony aware that his dream of the baby suckling at its mother's breast will never be fulfilled. He is coming to terms with the immutability of his family, his future and his despair.

t·h·r·e·e

TONY'S THERAPY: FLIRTING WITH DISASTER

Even though Tony's therapy occupies a relatively small percentage of the total screen time, it provides the audience with an opportunity to reflect on the central question of the series: Is Tony redeemable? The complexity of his inner world is evident in all of Tony's activities outside of therapy, but it is in Dr. Melfi's consulting room that he really confronts the discrepancy between who he wants to be and who he has become.

Dr. Melfi devises a rational treatment plan for Tony's panic attacks and depression. She prescribes Prozac, an antidepressant that improves both conditions. He appears less depressed, and his panic attacks abate, at least for the moment. His depression then worsens. He finds it hard to get out of bed, and Carmela is worried. Dr. Melfi augments the Prozac with lithium to give it a "kick start." Like many men who take Prozac in real life, Tony has problems with sexual performance. When his panic attacks persist, Dr. Melfi adds Xanax, another drug that is effective for panic disorders. The writers consult with a psychiatrist about the use of medications so their choices are accurate.

The therapy in *The Sopranos* departs from the conventions of cinematic psychiatry. Of some four hundred American films depicting mental health treatment, one is hard-pressed to find a single example of the effective prescription of psychotropic medications. The psychopharmacology revolution that occurred in psychiatry during the last three decades of the twentieth century never made its way onto the silver screen. Psychiatrists generally peddle the talking cure in movies, possibly because of its role in advancing the narrative and providing exposition.

Treating Tony Soprano with Prozac, on the other hand, clearly improves both his depression and his panic attacks. The only film that comes close to this positive depiction of psychopharmacology is the much praised 1997 film, *As Good as It Gets*, in which Jack Nicholson's obsessive-compulsive disorder appears to respond favorably to an unnamed medication. However, watching the film closely suggests an alternative argument: that it is the Helen Hunt character's love, not the medication, that makes the difference.

Combined with Tony's medication is twice-weekly psychoanalytic psychotherapy. The principles of this form of therapy are straightforward. The patient's childhood experiences are crucial to the understanding of his adult concerns. The therapist encourages the patient to view his behavior as having complex meanings that are largely unconscious and therefore require time to understand. Emotional problems have multiple determinants rather than a single cause. A young man who has difficulty accepting adult responsibility may be avoiding competition with his father, but he may also be worried that his mother will stop loving him if he stops being a needy child. In addition, he may feel that his success is destructive to his siblings.

The patient's feelings toward the therapist and the qualities he attributes to her are valuable sources of insights into meanings and causes because they reflect long-standing problematic patterns of relatedness. The same young man who is reluctant to grow up may feel that his female therapist wants him to stay dependent on her because he experienced his mother that way.

The therapist's counterpart to the patient's transference, known as countertransference, is a rich gold mine of information about what the patient evokes in others, not simply an obstacle or interference with the therapist's capacity to be objective. The therapist treating the young man who has trouble assuming responsibility may begin to feel protective and nurturant toward him and wish to shield him from the uncertainties of adult life. This feeling may reveal how her patient approaches women as well as reflecting a personality trait of the therapist herself. Indeed, in recent years the whole notion of therapeutic neutrality and objectivity has come under intense scrutiny. Today there is a consensus that the therapist's own personality has a strong influence on the shape of the patient's transference and contributes to what transpires in psychotherapy. The stone-faced, blank-screen analyst is now a relic of the past. Nevertheless, the treatment is still asymmetrical. One person pays a fee to another, so the patient's needs and interests must take center stage. The therapist is relatively less disclosing about her own life while encouraging the patient to free-associate—to say everything that comes to mind.

Psychoanalysis and psychoanalytic psychotherapy are the last strongholds of privacy in an electronic age. To expect a patient to say whatever comes to mind without censoring requires a context of airtight confidentiality. Only then can a patient believe that there are no negative consequences for openness. Even when privacy is assured, few patients can really come right out and say whatever thoughts emerge. A standard belief among analysts is that when patients can truly free-associate, they are ready to end the therapy! In *The Sopranos*, the principle of privacy is compromised in the very first session when Dr. Melfi interrupts Tony to present him with "ethical ground rules." She explains that she will have to contact the authorities if he reveals that someone is going to be killed or hurt. She knows from Dr. Cusemano that Tony is in the Mafia, and she doesn't want to be in a position of "ratting him out."

This so-called duty to warn has emerged in recent years as one of several exceptions to confidentiality—the others are the threat of suicide and an act of child abuse—that may force the therapist to violate the principle of confidentiality.

Is Dr. Melfi right to tell Tony about the limits of confidentiality? Probably so. At the same time, she is also squelching his capacity to reveal who he is to her. What ensues after her warning is a watered-down version of his life that is used to great comic effect by the writers. Tony reports, for example, that he had coffee with a man who owes him money. The flashback shows him running the guy down in his car. One can speculate that there are certain aspects of Tony's life that Dr. Melfi would prefer to avoid. Hence her cautionary statement to Tony may also reflect her anxiety about hearing unseemly details in the life of a mobster.

Tony must also compromise his own set of principles to see a psychiatrist. How can he talk about his personal problems without violating the Mob's code of silence? How can he gain insight into his problems without betraying his comrades? This setup has been described as an essential clash "between each culture's semiotic codes governing secrecy. Tony's is an outlaw culture relative to Jennifer's mainstream, professional, within-the-law culture. Both are nevertheless tightly bound to certain rules and roles, the dictates of which threaten the very fabric of the other's basic institution."

Right from the start, Tony's worries about confidentiality are strongly reinforced by Jennifer's dire warning. In a sham session he presents a fake life to avoid a privacy breach. He tells Dr. Melfi that he went to college for a semester and a half and understands all about psychotherapy and Freud. And he adds, "Where I come from, it doesn't go down."

Tony also undermines the therapy by immediately sexualizing the encounter. He calls Dr. Melfi "Hon" and tells her that his mother would have loved it if the two of them had gotten together. Noting her last name, he asks her what part of "the Boot" she's from. Although she maintains her professionalism, she does reveal the geographic origins of her father's family.

Dr. Melfi is flirting with disaster in this therapy on two counts. She must monitor her patient's every word to avoid dangerous consequences for both of them. From a mobster's perspective, there is no distinction between a therapist who is duty-bound to contact the authorities and a rat who squeals. Both deserve rat poison. She also must deal with Tony's challenging the professional boundaries inherent in the therapeutic relationship. She is fascinated by her celebrity "bad boy," and she must be careful not to collude with his wish to transform the therapy into flirtatious bantering or worse.

Tony, on the other hand, is tiptoeing on the brink of his own disaster. If word gets out that he sees a therapist—thus breaking the Mob's sacred code of silence—he could find himself wearing cement shoes off the coast of Jersey. In fact, his seeing a psychiatrist contributes to Uncle Junior's decision to have him killed.

These potential disasters force both therapist and patient into a silent pact from the first session. Their collusion is reminiscent of a famous analogy Freud used to illustrate the perils of allowing a patient to conceal information. He speculated about what would happen if a city assigned the right of asylum to one location. It would not take long, he noted, before "all the riff-raff of the town" gathered there. He even described his treatment of a high government official, who claimed he could not communicate certain thoughts because they contained state secrets. The analysis "came to grief" as a result. If an area of the patient's life is off limits to the analyst, all his shameful secrets and guilty pleasures may take shelter in that concealed sector of the psyche. Compartmentalization like this perfectly fits into Tony's vertically split psyche.

Given these perilous precautions, it shouldn't surprise us that the therapy gets off to a rocky start. But despite the collusion, things begin to happen. Dr. Melfi asks about his childhood. Prozac lifts his depression a bit. He finds himself quoting Dr. Melfi, often with humorous results. She compares the retirement center where Tony has placed his mother to a resort on Cap d'Antibes, and Tony later borrows her analogy but calls it "Captain Teebs."

It's difficult for Tony to see himself as a collaborator in a process of exploration, a recurring problem in the therapy. He is offended when Dr. Melfi suggests that he might have negative feelings toward his mother, and he ends many of the sessions by stomping out. Once he shouts, "I don't want to talk to you anymore. Hate your mother?" When Dr. Melfi suggests latent or unconscious meaning may be at odds with Tony's conscious views, he is outraged and declares, "You shrinks think everyone is lying to you." This statement is followed by, "Fuck you," Tony's equivalent of "Have a nice day," as he storms out of the office.

The audience begins to wonder if Tony will end up like Woody Allen's cinematic protagonists, who endure analysis for twenty years only to wind up in Lourdes. It doesn't help that Dr. Melfi is a bit formal and stuffy and that she some-times lapses into jargon: "I thought we made progress on your narcissism," she says stiffly.

Just when the situation begins to look hopeless, however, Tony gets the hots for his therapist. This transformation is her-alded by a dream in which the nether regions of Dr. Melfi's upper thigh are exposed, and she smiles seductively at Tony from her office chair. Later in the dream he approaches Dr. Melfi from behind, and when she swivels around in her desk chair, her face has morphed into that of Tony's mother, Livia. Tony is only slightly more shocked than if she had been the corpse of Norman Bates's mother, and he awakes with a start.

The message is clear. Tony has fallen in love with his ther-apist. He is deeply conflicted about it, though, because it feels incestuous to him. He seriously considers quitting and tells Carmela that therapy is too much exposure for him. At the same time, he conceals the therapist's gender from Carmela by using the male pronoun when talking about Dr. Melfi. As far as Tony is concerned, he is cheating on his wife because, like Jimmy Carter, he is lusting in his heart.

As he becomes more and more fascinated with his therapist, Tony feels compelled to find out more about her. Because the emphasis in therapy is on the patient's world, the therapist's life remains a mystery. Patients are usually curious, though, and many would love to have a daily report on their doctor's comings and goings. But only Tony Soprano has the moxie to put this fantasy into action. He hires crooked cop Vin Makasian (John Heard) to tail Dr. Melfi. Makasian reports that she works from eight to six, lives alone in a condo and sees her own shrink, Elliot Kupferberg, once a week. Most important to Tony, his informant assures him: "She don't fuck anyone."

Tony's voyeur-for-hire gets out of hand when he trails Dr. Melfi during a date with a man (played by Mark Blum) whom Vin describes as "not much in the balls department." Makasian then beats up Jennifer's date, and in the next therapy session, Dr. Melfi is clearly shaken by what has happened. She is more revealing of herself than ever as she tells Tony the details. The audience cheers as it starts to detect a role reversal: Tony is beginning to take care of his doctor. He empathizes with her feelings of outrage and asks if she is okay. Dr. Melfi responds by saying that the worst part of all of it is that her relationship with her boyfriend will never be the same. She suddenly realizes that she has begun to confide in her patient, and she says to him, "This is very unprofessional . . . it's your session." Tony tries to shore her up by telling her that he has gotten lots of good ideas in the therapy.

The term "professional boundary" refers to an "edge" of acceptable behavior in psychotherapy. Sessions take place in an office where two people sit in chairs and emphasize talk rather than action. One pays the other a fee for a service. Gifts are generally not exchanged. The two avoid business deals or anything else that would distract from the psychotherapeutic relationship. Although they have strong feelings toward one another, they do not engage in a sexual relationship. Generally, the therapist does not talk about her personal problems with the patient because it is his dime. This set of professional boundaries also defines the therapist's professional role and differentiates it from a friend or a lover.

A flexible and effective psychotherapist sometimes bends the boundaries a bit in ways that are not necessarily harmful to the patient. These boundary *crossings* are usually brief and attenuated, and the patient and therapist are able to talk openly about them. By contrast, boundary *violations* are egregious and destructive transgressions of professional boundaries that may ultimately seriously undermine the therapy. Sexual contact between therapist and patient is one example. The ethics codes of all professional mental health organizations forbid therapist–patient sex because it exploits the patient's vulnerability and destroys the therapy.

Dr. Melfi's role reversal is an example of a boundary crossing. She uses Tony to ventilate about her own private situation, recognizes that she has overstepped the bounds and steps back. One of the authentic aspects about her character is that she's shown struggling with her feelings toward Tony, but making a genuine effort to keep these feelings under control and channel them productively into the therapy process. Moreover, she uses her own therapy with Elliot to understand her countertransference and harness it in the service of Tony's treatment.

Although movie audiences may never know it, we therapists rely heavily on our own therapy to understand what happens with our patients. I remember vividly how helpful my own analyst was when I was treating a celebrity patient early in my career. As day after day I recounted my fascination with my patient's extraordinary life, my analyst finally put things in perspective: "You know, sometimes I think you are so entertained by him that you may forget that you are there to help him understand why he is so miserable."

By episode six of the first season, despite his protestations about the uselessness of therapy, Tony has clearly fallen in love with his therapist. Therapeutically speaking, this is not a bad thing. In a 1906 letter to Jung, Freud said, "Essentially, one might say, the cure is effected by love." He did not mean the therapist's love for the patient but rather the patient's transference love for the doctor. We see Tony regularly experiencing erotic dreams about Dr. Melfi. In one he is lying in his bed while Jennifer is fellating him to the tune of "What time is it? It's time for love." He then sees Jennifer's face and wakes up with a start. Carmela accuses him of being uninterested in lovemaking. He attributes this to the Prozac, but the truth is he is saving himself for his therapist. He dreams of Jennifer coming out of the shower nude and saying, "Mr. Soprano," beckoning him into her new office.

Carmela senses the erotic attraction and confides in Father Phil (Paul Schulze), her somewhat unctuous but emotionally available parish priest, that for the first time she feels Tony is being unfaithful to her. It is not uncommon for the spouse of a therapy patient to feel excluded and jealous. Like many wives, Carmela wonders why Tony can't talk to her about his problems.

Finally, Tony can no longer contain himself. He tells his therapist that she is "soft, like a mandolin," and he walks over to her and tries to kiss her. She places her hand between her face and Tony's to fend off the kiss and then stands up. She notes that their time is up and suggests that he might come back in the afternoon so they can discuss what just happened. Tony declines and leaves with his tail between his legs, feeling unloved and unwanted.

The sexual boundary is one that Jennifer has no intention of crossing, but her excitement about Tony seeps through in her behavior. She hesitates a moment too long when he tries to kiss her, so that his lips virtually touch hers. Even the ambiguity of her suggestion that Tony should come back in the afternoon could be construed as reflecting sexual interest. Indeed, *Sopranos* writer Robin Green regrets the line and wishes she could go back and change it, but Jennifer's mixed message lets both the audience and Tony know that she is ambivalent about the professional boundaries.

When Tony returns for his next session, he explains to Dr. Melfi, "I'm in love with you. I'm sorry. That's just the way it is. I dream about you. I think about you all the time. I can't get excited about any other woman." Jennifer's response is professional rather than personal. She explains to him that he feels that way because the therapy is going well. Tony is hurt once again and lets his doctor know that he doesn't like being made a mama's boy and thinks that Freud's idea about every boy wanting to have sex with his mother is "crap." Why can't she see his love as simply what he feels in his heart?

Here Dr. Melfi makes a common but fundamental error. She implies that the love Tony feels for her is not "real." From the patient's perspective, love for the therapist feels extraordinarily real, and the therapist's failure to validate the patient's experience of it can be experienced as a devastating dismissal. Feeling misunderstood, some patients will decide not to bring up their longings ever again, whereas others, like Tony, will make a beeline for the door.

After stomping out of Melfi's office, he confides in Carmela, "This psychiatry shit. Apparently what you're feeling is not what you're feeling. And what you're not feeling is your real agenda." Even though she admits her jealousy, Carmela pleads with Tony to continue. She acknowledges that she envies Dr. Melfi's ability to help Tony because she wants to be the woman that Tony turns to for help. In a tender moment Tony reassures her of his love for her.

What is going on here? Is this an accurate account of psychoanalytic psychotherapy? Or a spoof of daytime drama? Freud knew long ago that an analyst who listens quietly and empathically to her patient will eventually encounter love as the most powerful obstacle to continuing the treatment. After all, Tony's wish to make passionate love to Jennifer has become far more important to him than addressing his panic attacks. However, it was Freud's genius to realize that when a patient falls in love with a therapist, it is not simply a resistance to the treatment process, but a revelation of important patterns of old relationships being brought into the present. Indeed, it *is* the treatment. All Tony's complicated feelings about Livia, Carmela, his Russian goomah Irina (Oksana Babiy) and even Meadow are revealing themselves in the emerging relationship with his therapist. If he can tolerate the frustration long enough to use the potential insights from his erotic transference, he can begin to understand the meanings of his attachment to Dr. Melfi. Drawing attention to how much she has in common with Tony's wife, mother and daughter, Jennifer suggests, "Maybe by coming clean with me you're dialoging with them."

Anyone who has been in psychotherapy can relate to this phenomenon. The consulting room is a stage onto which a cast of characters emerge from the wings and cross the floor-boards. They make their appearance in the relationship with the therapist. As the patient brings up emotional baggage related to his father, that father becomes alive in the way he relates to the doctor. When he speaks of his mother, she "appears" in the play space between the patient and therapist.

Despite his penchant for malapropisms, Tony is no fool, and his frustration is particularly difficult for him to bear because he can tell that Jennifer finds him enticing. He confronts her. "Why do you have me as a patient? Most legit people I know would go a hundred miles out of their way not to have eye contact with me. But you, you didn't flinch." Dr. Melfi is taken aback and looks down with an expression of shame. Tony is on to her. There is no place to hide in therapy.

The writers wisely chose to preserve Dr. Melfi's fundamental competence as a psychiatrist while humanizing her as a lonely divorcee fascinated by her patient. Nowhere in American cinema or television have audiences ever witnessed the erotic tension that emerges in therapy handled so credibly. Since the 1940s, cinematic mythology has tacitly agreed that a woman therapist cannot maintain her professionalism in the face of a handsome and sexy male patient. In the Hollywood version of psychotherapy, the scalps of female therapists have adorned the bedposts of male patients for decades. Ingrid Bergman succumbed to Gregory Peck in *Spellbound*. Mai Zetterling gave up her profession to marry Danny Kaye in *Knock on Wood*. Natalie Wood jumped into bed with Tony

Curtis in *Sex and the Single Girl*. Julie Andrews could not resist the overtures of her womanizing narcissistic patient (Burt Reynolds) in *The Man Who Loved Women*. Lena Olin surrendered her license so she could sit on rooftops with manic-depressive Richard Gere in *Mr. Jones* (1992). And in *Tin Cup* (1996), René Russo, who has given up real estate to become a psychotherapist, finds her patient and golf teacher (Kevin Costner) irresistible.

This trend runs throughout film history, completely untouched by feminism. Twice as many women therapists in American film sleep with their male patients as male cinematic therapists who sleep with women patients. Of course, this is exactly the opposite of real life: Ethics committees find that for every female therapist who has violated sexual boundaries, there are three or four male therapists.

Decades of these portrayals have set up the audience to expect the same thing to happen in *The Sopranos*. Indeed, the writers and producers were deluged with letters asking why Tony and Jennifer didn't just go ahead and get it over with. Audiences could care less about ethics codes. They want to see traditional gender roles restored—Tony as Tarzan and Jennifer as Jane. As Tony says, "You're a woman. I'm a man. End of story."

Chase and his writing crew have deftly raised expectations by depicting Dr. Melfi in the usual situation of women therapists in the movies—divorced and unfulfilled. She appears to be a workaholic without much of a love life. Of particular interest is Chase's casting of Lorraine Bracco in the role. Viewers automatically associate her with the part she played in Martin Scorsese's *GoodFellas*. In that film she played the classic Mafia wife, married to mobster Henry Hill (Ray Liotta). In fact, that's where Chase spotted her. Even though she plays Jennifer Melfi with consummate skill, the twinkle in her eye reminds us of her previous role. In one conversation with her "not-much-in-the-balls-department" boyfriend, they are talking about maleness and femaleness. Jennifer laments that men are going into the woods and beating drums. Her boyfriend suggests, "You want someone sensitive to your needs but still decisive enough for the occasional grope in the closet." She smiles and acknowledges that he's on to something.

We are led to believe that Tony Soprano is the kind of decisive man Jennifer needs, especially compared to her traumatized boyfriend, who is afraid to leave the house since he took a beating from Tony's man. The audience has no doubt which of the two is game for a grope in the closet. Nowhere is this more clearly suggested than in the Emmy-winning "Employee of the Month" episode. At the beginning of the episode, Dr. Melfi is living with her ex-husband, Richard, again. As usual, he is highly critical of her effort to treat Tony and quips, "Hollywood tries to give these sociopaths the tragic grandeur of Al Pacino." (The writers are never reluctant to poke fun at themselves.) When Jennifer says that Tony has had a breakthrough, Richard replies with contempt, "Break through what? Somebody's jaw?"

In this same episode she is brutally raped on her way to the parking garage, only to have the police foul up so that the rapist is allowed to go free. She later sees the rapist's photograph on the wall of a fast food restaurant where he has received the "employee of the month" award. Jennifer tries to talk to Richard, but he is completely useless. She blames Richard for reacting to the news that the rapist had an Italian name, and he blames her because she did not call security before she went to the garage. Later Richard says he wishes he could "find that bastard and kill him with these hands. I could, and I would, but I can't. They'd put me in jail. That's how messed up things are." Jennifer, longing for vigilante justice, says, "I know." The camera then cuts to Tony splitting a log in two with an ax. Like Jennifer, the viewer knows there *is* a man who can take justice into his hands.

Dr. Melfi's unconscious is clear on the role she would like Tony to play in her life. She dreams that she is sitting at her desk. She rises and goes to double doors that say "Danger High Voltage." She opens the doors and enters a room with a soda machine. She places two dry macaronis in the slot but can't get her can of soda out. She hears a dog growling and turns around to see a rottweiler. The rapist walks in behind her and grabs her. The rottweiler comes to the rescue and attacks the rapist, who screams.

In the next scene she is talking with her therapist, Elliot, about the sense of relief she felt in the dream. Elliot suggests that the dog was "the forbidden part of your psyche—murderous rage." Jennifer corrects him by saying at first she thought the dog was after her. Elliot reminds her that the doors said "Danger." Jennifer, experiencing a memory lapse, retorts, "No, actually it said 'High Voltage.'" Her meaningful forgetting of the word "Danger" helps the audience understand that in her fascination with Tony, she is willing to overlook his dangerous side and focus on him as protector.

Women who involve themselves with antisocial men often have a remarkable capacity to disavow the danger. Because these men seem tough and macho, women attracted to them describe how "safe" they feel in their company. Their own attraction to danger is often split off and disavowed, just as Jennifer's dream suggests.

In fact, in my clinical experience, most women therapists who actually become sexually involved with their male patients fit the scenario suggested by *The Sopranos*. A charming rogue, usually with a severe personality disorder, has charmed his therapist into thinking that he is really a softie underneath. She sees the patient as a baby who needs the love of a good woman to settle him down. She imagines that in return she will have ecstatic sex and a sense of safety that other men cannot give her.

Dr. Melfi's unconscious is working in exactly this direction. In her session with Elliot, she points out that the dog, a rottweiler, is a direct descendant of the dog used by the Roman army to guard their camps—a dog with a big head and massive shoulders. As she free associates to this image, she is stunned by a sense of recognition: "I'm digging. Who do I dig with? And who's dangerous? Who could I sic on that son of a bitch to tear him to shreds?" Then with her voice trembling, she speaks of the rapist: "Let me tell you something. No feeling has ever been so sweet as to see that pig beg and plead and scream for his life, because the justice system is fucked up." Scornfully, she says that Richard has a $300-an-hour attorney looking into it, but "that Employee-of-the-Month cocksucker is back on the street, and who's going to stop him? You?" Elliot becomes concerned, but she reassures him that she won't break the "social compact." Then she clarifies, reminding him that it gives her a "certain satisfaction" to know that she could get rid of him if she wanted to.

The audience is one hundred percent behind Jennifer. When she was raped, viewers were viscerally affected: Colleagues of mine said they felt like it had happened to them or to a friend. So the rape drives *The Sopranos* audience into a feeding frenzy. They are dying for Melfi to use her transference power over Tony to have him rub out the rapist. In the last scene of the episode, she begins to cry, and Tony goes over to her and puts his arm around her to comfort her. She talks through her tears and asks him to sit down again. Tony asks, "You want to say something?" The viewers, now on their feet screaming "Yes!" are clamoring for Jennifer to authorize the whack. Instead, she says, "No." The screen goes to blackout, and we realize that the writers have once again defied cinematic convention and maintained her principled stand.

As the "no" resonates in the silence, we feel ashamed at how bloodthirsty and barbaric we have become. Lorraine Bracco reports that people came up to her on the street for months afterwards asking her, "Why didn't you tell him?" David Chase, who took flak for the violent realism in the rape episode, defends his choice: "In order for us to understand the principled stance she takes, you have to see how brutally bad the rape was."

In fact, the original story line had Tony arranging to have the rapist killed. However, the writers decided that although the audience's blood lust for revenge would have been satisfied, the therapeutic relationship would have been finished. One of the consistent virtues of *The Sopranos* is that the writing is character-driven. It would not have been in Jennifer's character to exploit the transference relationship to place her own needs above those of her patient.

Of course, the fact that Dr. Melfi is principled could have been fatal to the series. People of high moral character can be terribly boring. Compare Michael Dukakis to Bill Clinton. Fortunately, Jennifer is sufficiently titillated by her rottweiler, though, that she keeps us guessing if she can tiptoe along the abyss of boundary violations without falling over the edge. She lets it slip at a family dinner that she's treating a mobster. When Tony's neighbors, the Cusemanos, invite her over for an evening, she sneaks off to the bathroom. She can't quite see her patient's house from the window, so she stands on the bidet for a better view. At the same dinner party, the guests ridicule the Sopranos for having Murano glass on their bar. Jennifer stops their laughter cold with a terse: "I like Murano glass."

The morning after her peeping episode, Tony happens to bring up Frank Cusemano in the course of the session and refers to him as "a Wonder Bread Wop." As the session ends, and Tony strides toward the door, Jennifer can't resist telling him that she was next door the previous night. She even asks him if he heard anyone scream out in pain. (In fact, the scream came from Tony's exertion while lifting weights.)

A therapist—or a patient—watching this episode would wonder why Melfi made such a revelation at the very end of the hour. Tony is equally puzzled. For both patient and therapist, the "exit line" at the door may reveal feelings that have been latent during the session and that now burst forth freely. Both patient and therapist create an artificial partition between the session proper and the few moments of entrance and exit. Getting out of the chair and walking to the door has a disinhibiting effect. Melfi is once again signaling her fascination with Tony, and he gets the message.

When she crosses her legs, her thighs are not the only things showing. Her unconscious regularly leaks out. These cracks in her professional façade draw us in and make us wonder how far she'll go. After suggesting that Tony keep a record of his panic attacks, she begins a session by asking him if he brought his log. Her deadpan expression suggests that she misses the double entendre. But Tony doesn't; he replies with a chuckle, "My log?"

Patients love to see the therapist's unconscious leak out because it confirms that they are having an impact on the therapist. Despite the professional boundaries, psychotherapy is a real relationship in which each partner affects the other. One of my most memorable exit lines occurred after I had been seeing an attractive woman in analysis for a couple of years. She sexualized sessions to the point where the erotic tension in the room was palpable. As she got up to leave my office, I clarified the schedule in light of my upcoming vacation: "So for the next two weeks, we will be having *sex* sessions instead of eight." She looked puzzled; I turned crimson. Neither of us was unaffected by my gaffe.

When Jennifer begins to medicate her anxieties with Ativan and a generous snort of Belvedere vodka before her sessions with Tony, she loosens up. Neuroanatomists and psychoanalysts have long known that the superego is that part of the brain that is soluble in alcohol. And Jennifer's drinking doesn't stop at her office door. One night she runs into Tony at a restaurant and can't resist going over to him. With a goofy schoolgirl grin, she greets him in a way that suggests he must be her favorite patient or her high school boyfriend.

Tony is perplexed by these chinks in Jennifer's professional armor because he's noticed that her boundary transgressions always stop short of disaster. For example, like most psychoanalysts, she charges him when he misses a session. Tony is enraged at what he sees as a scam. He literally throws his cash at her and contemptuously tells her that he's been pouring his heart out to "a fuckin' call girl." She responds by saying that she doesn't appreciate being made to feel afraid. Tony is deeply wounded and tells her that "it's obvious you don't give a shit about me or my situation. Otherwise, you wouldn't be shaking me down. Stick it up your ass." Once again, he storms out, letting her know that he can play the exit-line game also.

The message Tony receives is that he must pay for caring. The comparison to a prostitute is familiar to therapists because psychotherapy presents a conundrum. The therapist may genuinely care about the patient. But would she care if payment were not involved and it were not a professional relationship? No one can say for sure, so the patient continues to be vexed by the possibility that the therapist might not have anything to do with him if they had met in another setting.

Dr. Melfi's tantalizing unavailability activates the tremendous rage Tony has for his mother, Livia. She, too, was never available to him in the way he wanted her to be; the explosion at Jennifer is aimed at Livia for past wounds and Jennifer for present ones. In an interview about her character, Lorraine Bracco noted, "I think it's that whole I'm-not-available thing. I believe it's one of the great reasons it works. . . . One, I am his equal, I'm as powerful as he is, and two, besides the sexuality, he's so attracted to her because she's so much smarter than him, and knowledge is seductive."

The analogy between a therapist and a prostitute is taken further when Tony visits a madam in a brothel to talk about his hit man, Vin Makasian, after he commits suicide. Tony even asks her if Vin came there for therapy. The madam acknowledges that she trades the couch for a bed, and she looks at Tony and says, "Who wouldn't want to sleep with their shrink?"

Dr. Melfi's attraction to danger, and her titillation at treating a Mafia don, reaches its peak after Tony narrowly survives the hit ordered by Junior. We see Carmela and Tony at night in an unidentified location. Jennifer drives up in her car, and Tony gets into the front seat with her. He asks if she has ever told anyone about his treatment. She tells him that she told her family she had someone in the Mob in treatment but never mentioned his name or any other identifying features. He lets her know that he has been mobilized by the botched attempt on his life. He reminds her of a time in therapy when he said he didn't want to live. Now he says he doesn't want to die and that he is frightened. Using his therapist's car as a mobile office, he recalls his hallucination of the baby suckling at the voluptuous mother's breast. Jennifer points out that the baby was Tony, and the memory represented a wish to be nursed by a loving mother. This interpretation brings Tony to tears.

Would a psychotherapist drive out to a deserted road in the middle of the night to meet her patient in her car? It would certainly be a remarkable boundary crossing, but the treatment of a Mafia don would also be extraordinary. To Dr. Melfi's credit, she is all business during the meeting and tries to help him understand his longings in the middle of a traumatic event.

Viewers who thought that the crisis might finally propel Dr. Melfi into her patient's arms are once again frustrated. For the show's creators, having Dr. Melfi sleep with Tony was never even a remote consideration. Chase found the very prospect unthinkable. When asked if Tony and Dr. Melfi would ever sleep together, he replied, "Ludicrous. . . . The hiding and shame is not what the show's about, and the therapy would be ruined." In fact, Lorraine Bracco made it clear that she was interested in playing Dr. Melfi only if the therapy was respected. She told Chase, "If you're going to make her a drug-crazed, psychotic killer sex addict, I won't do it." Therapy had helped her a great deal, and she did not want to see it mocked.

A patient who sleeps with his therapist commits symbolic incest. The nature of transference is such that any man in therapy with a woman will begin to experience his therapist as though she were his mother. The successful seduction of the therapist is not simply a violation of the therapist's ethics code. It also represents a fulfillment of the childhood wish to have Mother to oneself and usurp Father. The patient who fulfills that wish may feel temporarily triumphant, but over time the victory is replaced with guilt feelings and intense anxiety about possible retaliation.

In the few case reports of boys who have had sexual relations with their mothers, the long-term impact is substantial. Most of these people come to treatment as adults because they suffer from a chronic sense of dread. Some are convinced that lightning will strike at any moment and that they will be punished for their transgressions.

The writers of *The Sopranos* find the symbolic oedipal transgression unacceptable, but they are acutely tuned in to the viewers' prurient longings. We don't want to see therapists behaving themselves. This isn't reality—this is HBO! Thus, the show depicts the forbidden coupling in one of Tony's dreams. He appears in Dr. Melfi's waiting room in his undershirt and with a two-day growth of beard. When he gets up to enter her office, his erection is visible under his pants. He forcefully takes her on her desk, not only fulfilling his own lust but also satisfying the needs of millions of viewers who can no longer abide the thought of such an ethical female therapist. With tongue partially in cheek, though, the writers pull the rug out from under the celebrating viewers by waking Tony up from his feverish vision. The storytelling conveys a powerful message: Only in your dreams, guys. Only in your dreams.

Ultimately, it is violence, not sex, that disrupts the therapy. Confident that she is making headway after her automotive therapy session, Dr. Melfi tells Tony that his "subconscious" was shouting something at him during the hallucination of the mother and baby. As she continues to press Tony to face the fact that a wannabe Oedipus is dealing with a wannabe Medea, Tony starts to get the picture. Does she mean that his mother wanted him dead? he asks her.

Jennifer, on a roll, reminds him that in his worst dream a duck flies off with his penis, and she adds that at the very best his mother has borderline personality disorder. She then grabs the official handbook of psychiatric diagnosis, always within reach, and methodically explains how the diagnostic criteria apply to Livia.

Tony is not in the mood for a lecture, and he explodes, turning over the table in Dr. Melfi's office and grabbing her by the collar. With barely suppressed rage he says, "That's my mother—not some banana who stabbed you in the shower." He wants her to know that he's not Norman Bates and his mother has nothing in common with Norman's poor mother.

Behavior like this usually signals that the patient isn't suited for psychoanalytic therapy. As Jennifer tells Elliot, "Richard was right. I've been charmed by a sociopath." When Tony returns later that day, she starts to call 911, but he gives his word that she's in no physical danger. Hoping that just maybe Tony, like O. J. Simpson, is a nice guy who's been victimized by the media, Jennifer lets him in her office. But she keeps a pair of scissors up her sleeve, just in case. The reason a hit was ordered on him, Tony tells her, is that he's seeing a shrink. Genuinely worried, Jennifer assures him that she's ethically bound not to reveal anything about him to anyone. Tony is unimpressed and insists that Jennifer leave town because she's in danger. By now completely terrified, her response is, "Jesus fucking Christ! I have patients! Some of them are suicidal." So the first season ends with the therapy disrupted, Jennifer on vacation, one hopes in one of the top ten resorts endorsed by the government's witness protection program, and Tony wondering if he'd be better off sending E-mails to a cybershrink on Here2Listen.com.

$f \cdot o \cdot u \cdot r$

IS TONY TREATABLE?

At the end of the first season the outcome of the psychotherapy is hard to assess. Is it a complete failure? Is it possible to pick up the pieces after a patient turns a table over and grabs you by the collar? Was Dr. Melfi really making headway before the therapy ended? Is there a glimmer of hope in his wish to protect her?

Someone with as many antisocial traits as Tony is not realistically going to show dramatic changes in the first year of therapy. Much of the therapist's task is to help the patient reflect on chronic patterns of behavior that are embedded in his character and that he thus takes for granted. These traits, which are so much a part of the person that they do not create distress, must be transformed so that they begin to make him uncomfortable. The therapist needs time to convince the patient that his habitual behavior is going to land him in some kind of emotional trouble. Hence in an ordinary therapy we would not expect Tony to show great improvement in his insight or behavior, even though his panic attacks may have improved considerably with a combination of medication and psychotherapy.

Most of us aren't that interested in insight. We go to a therapist because we are suffering. If our symptoms of anxiety or depression lift, we may feel reluctant to examine our behavior in enough depth that we start to feel distress about its consequences. Insight is often more the therapist's agenda than the patient's. No matter what we may profess at the beginning of therapy, most of us would rather be loved or validated than have our behavior scrutinized under a microscope.

Dr. Melfi's motivation for treating Tony is murky. Is her wish to help him driven by a need to rescue a man who is beyond redemption? Is there a subtle form of omnipotence in her professional dedication to her patient? Is her personal life so bereft that she treats Tony to gain the excitement and erotic titillation that she misses at home? Is a "charming sociopath" better than a boyfriend so tormented by stress that he cannot leave his house or an ex-husband who lectures her on morality?

It is a testament to the authenticity of *The Sopranos* that these questions are not easily answered. The analyst's motives, just like the patient's, are partly unconscious. A self-scrutinizing therapist's business-as-usual professional agenda may overlay darker, more complicated personal motives fueled by persisting childhood wishes and fears. I once served as a consultant to a therapist treating a young woman who was starving herself to death. In the course of the consultation, the therapist recognized that her devotion to her patient was in part an attempt to rescue her own mother, who had practically wasted away when she refused treatment for her depression. Psychoanalytic treatment is not practiced in an ambience of "either/or"—treatment always takes place in the land of "both/and."

So it is with Dr. Melfi. After threats on her life, we find her seeing patients at the Anthony Wayne Motel, where she has ensconced herself to preserve her safety. A male patient is leaving her motel room, and we can't help noticing a king-size bed that takes up much of the room. One can only imagine the fantasies stirred up in Dr. Melfi's patients by her Motel 6 school of psychotherapy. Her patient, who is less than thrilled with the setting, asks, "When is your new office ready?" She replies that the new carpet isn't in yet. He pointedly tells her that his old therapist worked out of his home. She says that's not convenient for her. As preposterous as this setup may seem to the steadfast viewers of *The Sopranos*, there is a tradition for it. The esteemed British analyst Melanie Klein used to take her patients along on her holidays in the Black Forest. Since she couldn't really take her analytic couch along with her, she conducted sessions in her hotel room, inviting her male patients to lie on her bed while she sat next to them. She must have wondered why their thoughts were so dominated by sex.

Meanwhile, Dr. Melfi is tormented by the loss of a patient to suicide during the time she was forced to abandon her office. She is furious with Tony, who has brought this misery on her. Tony doesn't give up easily, though, and surprises Dr. Melfi in a roadside diner, where he asks her to take him back. She lets him have the full force of her anger and informs him that he is responsible for her patient's suicide. When Jennifer tells him "Fuck you!" a phrase not recommended in most textbooks on psychoanalytic technique, Tony starts to get the idea that his therapy may be in jeopardy, and he asks for a referral. Dr. Melfi's response: "I would never ask another colleague to get involved with this. . . . Get out of my life!"

Just when viewers began to worry that the therapy might really be over, Dr. Melfi is shown agonizing in her own therapy with Elliot, feeling she has abandoned Tony and needs to make reparation. She tells Elliot about the time she greeted Tony in a restaurant while mildly inebriated after an evening with her girlfriends. She is mortified by her impulsive interaction with her former patient, and particularly by her way of saying good-bye to him: "Toodle-oo!"

Elliot asks her what was so wrong with "Toodle-oo"? (or, as she says, in total mortification, "Toodle fuckin' oo").

She tells him that this is not the way she talks, that it had to be someone else speaking.

But Elliot won't buy this. "It was Jennifer," he reminds her. "For whatever reason at that moment, you felt safer showing him Jennifer, not doctor."

Elliot then helps her see that another part of her would like to continue a different kind of relationship with Tony. Jennifer realizes that "young girls are not accountable for their behavior. I think toodle-oo was the action of a ditzy young girl, and I regressed into the girl thing to escape responsibility for abandoning a patient. He asked me for help."

Dr. Melfi then gets desperate for some sign from Elliot that she should not feel guilty. She pleads with him to reassure her that she did the right thing.

Elliot responds, "You gotta ask yourself why you became a psychiatrist in the first place. If it was only to help people to stop smoking or biting their nails, then so be it! Nothing wrong with that."

Jennifer reflects a moment and comments, "I don't know . . . the patient who committed suicide because I was treating this man, because I had to go on the lam."

Elliot responds, "Did you say 'lam'?"

In his simple reference to Mob jargon, Elliot recognizes that Tony has invaded Jennifer. He has gotten under her skin in such a way that she cannot extricate herself from him. While out of one side of his mouth Elliot attempts to absolve her of guilt, out of the other side, he suggests that a dedicated psychiatrist would continue her therapeutic efforts. Jennifer has become strongly identified with Tony, and she feels terribly guilty that she has let him down. This same episode ends when Jennifer has a provocative dream in which Tony is driving and begins to perspire as he starts to feel faint. He looks at

his Prozac bottle and finds it empty before losing consciousness. He passes out at the wheel with *Wizard of Oz* music
playing in the background: "You're out of the woods . . ." Jennifer drives up to the scene of the wreck, and she sees Tony
lying on the hood of his car after having gone through the
windshield. His face is bloodied, and his hand is still clutching
his Prozac. As she approaches the scene of the accident, the
Wizard of Oz music changes to the Wicked Witch of the West
theme heralding her arrival. She looks on with horror. At that
moment she awakens from the dream and writes it down so
she can analyze it in her therapy with Elliot.

Dr. Melfi's intense feelings of responsibility are apparent in
the dream. Separation and abandonment are themes that run
throughout *The Wizard of Oz*. Dr. Melfi feels she has abandoned her patient and is culpable for his demise in the car
accident in the same way the Wicked Witch tries to destroy
Dorothy. In her next session with Elliot, she recalls watching
the film on television while hiding under a blanket with her
sister. Elliot gets her to admit that we watch scary movies to
"experience the thrill of being terrified without the consequences."

And he observes pointedly that he's worried she's getting
a vicarious thrill from treating a mobster. Jennifer reminds
him in a fury that it wasn't exactly vicarious, and then, taking
a leaf from Tony's book, she storms out of the office. When
she returns for her next session, she tells Elliot that she realizes she behaved just like her patient. She goes on to say that

seeing Tony again might be very therapeutic for her. Elliot tries to explain that Tony's therapy is not supposed to be therapeutic for her. He then asks if Jennifer has sexual feelings for her patient. After a long pause, she replies: "No. I have feelings. On a personal level. He can be such a little boy sometimes." OK, Jennifer. Whatever you say.

Like the audience, Dr. Melfi thinks Tony may be salvageable if she can find the key to understanding the "little boy" within him. With just the right approach, he might grow up, take responsibility for himself and become the good man he aspires to be. Jennifer's courageous return to treating Tony is in part based on her fascination with the "train wreck" before her and in part related to an altruistic zeal to save a soul that is not quite lost.

Of course, from the standpoint of the series, she must take him back since *The Sopranos* would be empty without the therapy scenes, but she needs to be bolstered by Ativan and alcohol to get through the sessions. As the therapy continues, the audience must grapple with the same issues as Dr. Melfi. Is Tony treatable? Is Jennifer engaging in the kind of "cheesy moral relativism" of which her ex-husband accuses her? Can therapy get through to someone with Tony's antisocial history?

Chase himself is clearly intent on raising this moral dilemma for the viewer: "I benefited a lot from psychotherapy, and yet I do believe there's a lot of excusing of bad behavior that goes on in therapy—the basic premise being 'Well, your parents were such bad parents. How could you have done otherwise but to kill that dog?' 'Cause they always take *your* side. And when you say, 'Aren't you going to tell me what a schmuck I am for doing that?' they say, 'Is that what you want me to tell you—that you're a schmuck?'"

Here Chase is giving voice to a problem inherent in therapy—can "bad behavior" be understood as growing out of conflict and adverse childhood experience without completely absolving the patient of responsibility for his actions? Of course it can. You are not responsible for what happened to you as a child. But you are responsible for what you do as an adult, no matter how much you are influenced by unconscious forces stemming from childhood experiences. A good therapist does not always take your side. She may at times empathize with your experience and validate that you have every right to feel the way you do. But she will also help you begin to see how you are active in re-creating your childhood as an adult, and she will confront you when she sees you doing it.

Although many professionals will argue with an alarming degree of certainty that Tony is not treatable, the question does not have a straightforward answer. Because he experiences anxiety, depression, conflict and the capacity for guilt, a strong argument can be made that it is possible to make contact with his conscience and maybe to dissuade him from further violence. When Meadow's high school soccer coach turns out to be sexually molesting her girlfriend, Tony is ready to order the hit, but his therapy with Dr. Melfi is clearly influential in determining the ultimate course of action, which is to allow the authorities to arrest the coach and let the criminal justice system take it from there.

The issue of Tony's treatability has been extensively debated in our *Slate* TV Club dialogues. My colleague Joel Whitebook asserts that Dr. Melfi has really never been clear about her therapeutic goals. He stresses that by recommending Sun Tzu's *The Art of War,* an ancient book of Chinese military strategy, to Tony, she is essentially helping him to improve his strategic attitude toward his life and work rather than to challenge it.

Another *Slate* colleague, Margaret Crastnopol, questions whether the treatment can possibly be viable unless Dr. Melfi is getting a bit more help than what Elliot is providing in their once-weekly sessions. She stresses that Jennifer would probably need an analysis three or four times a week to work out her countertransference feelings so that she would be sufficiently freed up from her own conflicts to concentrate on Tony's issues.

My third colleague, Phillip Ringstrom, feels optimistic about Tony's prognosis. Although he recognizes that Tony will not become an Eagle Scout, he stresses the fact that he can internalize aspects of the therapy and the therapist in a way that may modify his antisocial core. Ringstrom points out that not only did Tony avoid ordering a hit on the soccer coach, but he took no action to break the kneecaps of Meadow's African-

American/Jewish boyfriend Noah. Crastnopol is skeptical about whether there are any signs of Tony's internalizing the therapeutic experience.

Both Whitebook and Crastnopol view the patient as potentially treatable, but they see the deficiencies of the therapist as undermining the treatment. Whereas Whitebook argues that her therapeutic strategies suggest that she is trying to reinforce his approach to life, which is based entirely on power considerations, Crastnopol points out that she appears to have no systematic theoretical approach to Tony's character pathology. In other words, she is basically using ad hoc strategies based on pragmatic considerations.

I think my two colleagues are too harsh in their judgment of our fictional therapist. Given the formidable challenges presented by a patient with Tony's psychopathology, even the most well-trained therapist would be thrown from the saddle repeatedly. Each time she is dislodged, Melfi manages to find a way back onto the horse and to take command of the treatment once again. During the second season, she is particularly adept at helping Tony deal with the problems his two adolescent children present him. When A.J. discovers existentialism and argues that there are no absolutes, Dr. Melfi helps Tony see how he may contribute to A.J.'s feelings: "In your family, even motherhood is up for debate." Tony responds, "No, it's not. I teach him to love and respect and appreciate his mother." Jennifer confronts him: "What about your mother? . . . Has Anthony Jr. heard you say that your mother is 'dead to me'?" Tony sulks a bit at this question and responds that he doesn't know.

Jennifer persists, suggesting that talk like this could lead A.J. to embrace nihilistic ideas. Tony feels accused, but Jennifer clarifies: "When some people first realize that they are solely responsible for their decisions, actions and beliefs, and that death lies at the end of every road, they can be overcome with intense dread . . . dull, aching anger that leads them to conclude that the only absolute truth is death."

Tony pauses after hearing Jennifer's observation and finally resigns himself to the truth of it: "I think the kid's on to something."

Throughout the psychotherapy process, however imperfect, Dr. Melfi is helping Tony take responsibility for the climate he has created in his household. She will not collude with Tony's tendency to delude himself, and she insists on helping him see how he transmits ideas about the world to his children.

In the psychotherapy of people like Tony with serious personality disorders, one of the goals is to help the patient begin to *mentalize*. These patients often experience events as "just happening" to them, as though they are victims of fate rather than authors of their own experience. Mentalizing means perceiving and understanding that feelings, intentions, beliefs and desires motivate one's own and others' behavior.

These patients often have histories of childhood abuse and neglect that caused them to shut down any perception of an internal world. Someone like Tony, whose mother threatened to poke a fork through his eye, copes by refusing even to conceive of his mother's feelings, because it is too horrific to contemplate a mother who wants to do that kind of violence to her child. Moreover, the child must deny the hatred implied by the mother's murderous wishes because it would make the child see himself as unlovable or worthless.

These people grow up with a poorly developed sense of how internal states motivate their own behavior or that of others. Psychotherapy with these patients is designed to help them elaborate on their emotional states so they can begin to think about the origins and consequences of their own self-destructive behavior, both to themselves and to others.

Dr. Melfi repeatedly uses this strategy, often very effectively. In one poignant session, Tony discusses his gift of a car to his daughter. Meadow immediately recognized that the car belonged to a friend of hers and that the friend's father gave it to Tony as payment for a gambling debt. Tony says to his therapist, "I must have known that she'd know that it was this fuckin' kid Eric's car, and how I got it, and she'd freak out."

In the ensuing dialogue, Jennifer helps Tony mentalize. She begins by asking him why he gave Meadow the car if he knew she'd freak out. Tony says he doesn't know and then remarks that he's been trying to shield her from the realities of his life. But, he adds angrily, "So it becomes my fault that he lost his kid's car? I gotta look out for him 'cuz he's a sick bastard?"

Referring to his friend Artie's restaurant he adds, "No one's telling him to refuse a plate of fettuccini to some fat fuck that wanders in that's eating himself to death." Jennifer zeroes in: "Maybe that's what you were saying to your daughter. . . . Meadow's going to be going away to college next year . . . leaving the nest." Tony says, "Not those fuckin' ducks again." Jennifer continues, "Maybe you are preparing her for reality, teaching her to fly."

In this exchange, Dr. Melfi valiantly persists in helping Tony reflect on the meaning of his behavior. She suggests that unconscious motivations may determine his behavior.

By the third season of *The Sopranos*, Tony is beginning to take the treatment more seriously. He struggles with the loss of Big Pussy at Christmastime, reminiscing about how willingly Pussy played Santa. He even shows signs of trusting Jennifer enough to tell her things that were formerly off limits. He lets her know that his old friend Pussy worked for the Feds. Before long, Tony is sitting in his therapist's office crying and poignantly asking for help. He recognizes that A.J. is growing up to become a replica of himself. He knows he has failed with Jackie, Jr., and he is terrified that the same fate awaits A.J. Military school is out of the question because of A.J.'s panic attacks. He turns to Dr. Melfi: "How are we gonna save this kid?" Even the major derailment of the therapy by Tony's affair with Gloria Trillo (Annabella Sciorra) is ultimately channeled into the treatment in such a way that Tony gains some genuine insight into his problems with women. Dr. Melfi's efforts at helping Tony mentalize have started to pay off.

Most of us begin therapy by fighting the therapist. Our defenses are activated, and we do not welcome the observations of the doctor. We try to convince the therapist that we have suffered at the hands of others. We secretly hope that the therapist will side with us in blaming our mother, father, spouse, God or the hand of fate. Only with time do we mellow enough to look at our own contributions to our suffering. There is no "quick fix" for what ails the soul. We can appreciate how painful it is for Tony to finally come to terms with his own responsibility. Indeed none of us want to face it in ourselves.

Despite Tony's progress, Dr. Melfi is increasingly discouraged as he continues to have panic attacks, and she tells him that it would be a good idea to move on to "behavior modification therapy." This decision is encouraged by Elliot, who wonders if she should be treating Tony in the first place. She gives Tony a book entitled *Feel the Fear and Do It Anyway*. Tony's response is less than enthusiastic: "You gotta be fuckin' kidding me." Dr. Melfi acknowledges that the title leaves something to be desired, but she sticks to her recommendation.

Cognitive-behavior therapy—an approach that focuses on problematic thinking—is the non-pharmacological treatment that has been most extensively studied in panic disorder. At least in the short run, the results are impressive, although the long-term effectiveness is unknown. Although there is nothing inherently outrageous about prescribing such a treatment, Dr. Melfi hasn't carefully considered the impact it would have on Tony. Predictably, he feels that she is trying to get rid of him, and he is reluctant to start over with somebody new after his therapist has stayed with him through his brush with death and his resurrection. Jennifer knows she has been charmed by a shady character but is still intensely attracted to him. Handing him off to a cognitive-behavior therapist is one way to dilute the intensity of the heated feelings between them and extricate herself from what increasingly seems like an untenable situation.

After the rape, however, she recognizes how strong her need is for a powerful man to protect her. When Tony offers to walk her to the parking garage, she declines, but she later tells Elliot that she wanted to fall into his arms and cry. Tony has reluctantly accepted her referral and tells her that he is willing to go to see a cognitive-behavior therapist. Jennifer abruptly says, "No." He is puzzled since he has had the feeling that "I've been gettin' the boot." Jennifer then breaks down in tears, recognizing that she cannot bear to see him go, especially not at the moment that she most needs the protection of her rottweiler.

As Dr. Melfi becomes increasingly exasperated with the course of the therapy, she makes another radical suggestion that is even more ill-advised. She asks Tony to bring Carmela into the session with him. The reasons for Dr. Melfi's recommendation are obscure. As a general principle, a therapist who tries to bring a spouse into the session after establishing a trusting relationship through three years of therapy is asking for trouble. The spouse is bound to feel that the therapist is loyal to her long-standing patient and can't believe that her point of view will be heard and understood.

This is exactly what happens with Tony and Carmela. After an uneasy silence in their first session, Carmela starts to feel blamed. She confronts Dr. Melfi: "Oh, I get it. Is this how it works? You can't get any answers out of him so you start lookin' for someone else to point the finger at?" Things spiral downward from there. After a long pause, Dr. Melfi observes that both of them seem angry. Tony, who at first was defending his therapist, now turns on her: "You must have been at the top of your fuckin' class."

On the drive home, Carmela cries quietly and reflects back on the session, observing that Dr. Melfi took Tony's side on everything. She speculates that Tony and Dr. Melfi will have a good laugh at her expense at their next session together.

Given that Carmela has been intensely jealous of Tony's relationship with Dr. Melfi all along, this creation of a jealous triangle should have been entirely predictable. Carmela once told Father Phil that she had never really felt betrayed by Tony until he started seeing Dr. Melfi. Perhaps Dr. Melfi wishes to deintensify the relationship with Tony, and thus her motivations are similar to her decision to refer him to cognitive-behavior therapy. On the other hand, throughout the therapy, Jennifer struggles with a dilemma around the relative merits of blaming Livia for Tony's problems or helping him to take responsibility for his actions. Bringing in Carmela can be understood as a way that Dr. Melfi may have unconsciously been trying to deflect some of Tony's heat onto his wife.

Another possible motivation, also largely unconscious, would be that Carmela is brought into the therapy as a way of strengthening the therapeutic alliance between Tony and Jennifer. When two people can join in the scapegoating of a third, the "common enemy" brings them closer together. We've all seen this happen in our own families and our own work settings. Hence, to some degree, Jennifer's bringing Carmela into the therapy may be an attempt to cast her in the role of a current-day Livia who is responsible for Tony's problems. This strategy blows up in Jennifer's face, as even Tony turns against her by the end of the session.

One way of understanding the developments in this ill-fated attempt at seeing Carmela and Tony together is that Jennifer herself ends up enacting the role of the "bad mother." A basic tenet of psychoanalytic treatment is that patients are engaged in an ongoing effort to transform the therapist into a transference object—a person from the patient's past who is still very much alive as a haunting internal presence. Through Tony's behavior, he unconsciously gets Jennifer to fail him as his mother failed him. We all have friends and acquaintances who seem to repeat the same disastrous relationship scenario with myriad partners. Even though the names change, the same partner is created again and again.

Jennifer's sometimes erratic behavior in the therapy sessions can be partially understood as a mirror image of what happens inside Tony. Patients who have vertical splits tend to evoke reactions in therapists that correspond to the different sectors of the patient's psyche. Thus when Tony shows his contemptuous and antisocial colors, Dr. Melfi may become confrontative and even nasty in her responses to him. When, on the other hand, Tony sheds a tear and shows genuine concern, Jennifer becomes softer and gentler with him. This shifting of roles helps the therapist understand the patient's internal world more fully.

Dr. Melfi assures herself a chapter in *Great Moments in the Countertransference* when she double-schedules Tony and Gloria Trillo. Double-scheduling patients is relatively rare for therapists who are reasonably organized. Placing Mr. Womanizer and Ms. Slutola in the same waiting room at precisely the same moment could hardly be an accident. How do we understand this "scheduling error"? What is Jennifer up to? Although she may be attempting to diffuse the intensity of the countertransference as she did when she brought in Carmela, there are other possibilities to consider. Might Jennifer be acting out her own sexual wishes through her patient? In other words, Tony can deal with his erotic wishes toward Dr. Melfi by shifting them onto another gorgeous Italian woman of the same age, and Jennifer can vicariously hear the graphic descriptions of their trysts in Gloria's weekly session—if she shows up, that is. It's also conceivable that Jennifer is unconsciously setting up the situation so that Gloria can destroy the Sopranos' marriage.

This fiasco occurs when Jennifer is still in a posttraumatic state, filled with rage, longing to collapse and cry in Tony's arms. Her sessions with Elliot show us she is barely holding herself together, despite her composed appearance in the office. As if her judgment was not already a touch impaired, Jennifer then accepts extra money from Tony for the good week he has had with Gloria. In the course of the treatment she has gone from "therapist as prostitute" to "therapist as madam." She is taking her cut for setting him up with Gloria.

Dr. Melfi is furious about what is happening between her two patients. After Tony leaves the office, she talks with her son on the phone. She tells Jason that she hates all her patients because they lie to her face. Tony drops hints everywhere of Gloria's influence but won't acknowledge the relationship to his therapist. The smoking gun is Tony's parroting of Gloria's Buddhist observations.

"I joyfully participate in the suffering of the world," he declares. Jennifer notes that his comment has an Eastern flavor, to which Tony retorts, "Well, I've lived in Jersey all my life."

When Tony finally comes clean, he informs Jennifer that he has never felt better. He explains that Gloria makes him happy: "As much as I love my wife, being with Gloria makes me happier than all your Prozac and all your therapy bullshit combined." Most patients are secretly convinced that love is the real cure for their ills. If they can't get that love from their therapist, they will get it elsewhere. These triumphs are usually short-lived. As is the case with Tony, when you fly Euphoria Airlines, you always crash-land.

The romance between two patients places Jennifer in a delicate situation. By the standards of any ethics code, she cannot talk about one patient to another. She actually rises to the occasion by doing a good piece of work on the distinction between Tony's fantasies about Gloria and who she really is. Tony begins a session by asking Jennifer to tell him about Gloria's problems. She informs Tony about the constraints of confidentiality. Operating on the assumption that every woman has her price, Tony offers her an "additional five." Dr. Melfi declines and indicates that she's not charging him this month because of his large gratuity last month.

Tony then launches into his own observations about Gloria. He admires her independence. He notes that in contrast to Irina, who was a "helpless fuckin' baby," Gloria made her own way in the world and even went to Morocco by herself. He is mesmerized by her dark black eyes that remind him of a Spanish princess in a painting by "Goyim." Once again encouraging Tony to mentalize, Dr. Melfi asks Tony what might be going on in Gloria's mind that makes her attracted to Tony. He reflects for a moment: "With all the fuckin' faggots and crybabies runnin' around, I'm more of a captain of industry type."

Tony then applies the insights he has gained in treatment to his life outside the consulting room—the true test of the effectiveness of any psychotherapy. In the midst of a shouting match with Gloria, he has a blinding flash of insight worthy of Sophocles: "I didn't just meet you. I've known you my whole fuckin' life . . . my mother was just like . . . a bottomless black hole." Freud once commented that the finding of an object (psychoanalytic jargon for "person") is the *refinding* of it. Tony suddenly recognizes that he has refound Livia in the guise of a gorgeous Mercedes salesperson.

After this altercation, Tony agonizes in therapy about how Gloria actually wanted him to kill her. Dr. Melfi agrees that it was like "suicide by cop," and asks him, "How did you recognize in Gloria underneath all the layers of sophistication this deeply wounded angry being? That would let you replicate once again your relationship with your mother?"

Tony protests: "I don't want to fuck my mother. I don't give a shit what you say. You're never gonna convince me."

Jennifer persists: "Not 'fuck.' Try to please her. Try to win her love. . . . We need to repeat what's familiar even if it's bad for us. Gloria's need for dramas—the selfishness, the incessant self-regard. At one time in your mother's hands, it passed for love."

Dr. Melfi is on the mark. We are all destined to rerun the same internal scenarios in the private screening rooms of our minds. We even repeat scenarios that are abusive or painful exactly because we know them inside out and they provide a sense of continuity and even comfort. Tony Soprano becomes Everyman at this moment. Every viewer identifies with Tony's Sisyphean sentence to tread the same ground again and again.

The ultimate value of psychoanalytic therapy is not to eradicate that past. Neither is it to liberate the patient from the past. The goal is to bring the implications of the past fully into the conscious awareness of the patient so there is an increased capacity to choose a different path when confronted with the familiar old crossroads.

While Dr. Melfi flirts with disaster, not to mention with her patient, she somehow manages to back away from the edge of the precipice without falling into the abyss. We are never certain if she has successfully addressed her drinking problem, but she has persevered in the face of self-doubt and uncertainty about the "moral never-neverland" in which she finds herself. She has made an action-prone man who writes his own rules sit and reflect for awhile each week and learn that there are certain boundaries that won't be transgressed with her. The critic Ellen Willis captures her well: "In her person, the values of Freud and the Enlightenment are filtered through the cultural radical legacy of the 1960s: She is a woman challenging a man whose relationship to both legitimate and outlaw patriarchal hierarchies is in crisis. It's a shaky and vulnerable role, the danger of physical violence an undercurrent from the beginning, but there are also bonds that make the relationship possible." When Jennifer's ex-husband chides her about her moral relativism, he is missing the point. He fails to understand that only through the forging of a strong alliance with Tony does Jennifer have any chance of helping him examine his behavior. The way that Dr. Melfi rights herself after so many near misses suggests that at some fundamental level a moral compass is guiding her treatment and her relationship with Tony in a way that he has never experienced from any other woman in his life.

MEDEA, OEDIPUS AND OTHER FAMILY MYTHS

F ROM THE OPENING SCENE of the first episode, when Tony contemplates the breasts on the sculpture in Dr. Melfi's waiting room, we realize that his conflicts with his mother will be pivotal in *The Sopranos*. Anyone who has made a passing grade in Psychoanalysis 101 knows that a boy's relationship with his mother shapes all later relationships with women. One of the most poignant aspects of *The Sopranos* is Tony's never-ending search for a woman who will respond to him in the way that he longed for his mother to respond. Throughout the series the viewer, like Dr. Melfi, struggles with how much blame to attribute to Livia for her emotional and psychological abuse of Tony and how much of his contemptible behavior Tony must take responsibility for himself.

Ellen Willis calls Livia "Tony's heart of darkness," and she points out that although the series begins portraying her as simply a caricature of the complaining, nagging ethnic mother, she is "gradually revealed as a monstrous Medea." Most women would not appreciate this kind of comparison to a mythological figure. Aphrodite, yes; Medea, no. A woman who murders—or in Livia's case, attempts to murder—her children occupies a special category in the American psyche. The chilling accounts of Susan Smith in North Carolina and Andrea Yates in Texas fascinate us. The fact that the death penalty was even considered in the Yates case reflects the collective wish of many observers to obliterate the act of infanticide from our consciousness.

Mothers need to distance themselves from child murderers because of the shame and fear all mothers feel about the hateful impulses they have toward their babies. Psychoanalyst and pediatrician D. W. Winnicott once noted that there are at least eighteen reasons why a mother hates her baby from the beginning. Among these: The baby interferes with the mother's private life; the baby endangers the mother's body during pregnancy and delivery; the baby hurts her nipples when nursing; the baby treats the mother as a slave or an unpaid servant; and the baby ultimately is disillusioned with the mother. Despite Winnicott's noble efforts to normalize maternal hatred, destructive wishes toward one's own child are among the most disavowed and repressed of all human feelings. Hence when a mother actually takes the lives of her children, she has transgressed a taboo linked to a primal anxiety in mothers everywhere. When I attended a powerfully staged production of Euripides' *Medea* some years ago, six women in the audience stood up and walked out of the theater when the bodies of Medea's children were brought onto the stage.

The judicious use of flashbacks provides *The Sopranos'* audience with a sense of Tony's childhood traumas at the hands of Livia. In one vivid scene she threatens to gouge his eyes out with a fork when Tony begs her to buy him an electric organ. This threat, of course, brings to mind another Greek tragedy, one by Sophocles rather than Euripides. In *Oedipus Rex*, the protagonist blinds himself for having killed his father and taken his mother for himself. Freud viewed the blinding of Oedipus as a symbolic form of castration. The classical formulation of the Oedipus complex understands castration anxiety as stemming from the little boy's fear that his father will retaliate against him for his incestuous sexual wishes toward his mother and his murderous wishes toward his father.

Castration themes are everywhere in *The Sopranos*, beginning when Tony tells Dr. Melfi the dream in which his penis falls off. In a flashback from his childhood, Tony witnesses his father cutting off the finger of a butcher who owes him money. When Tony tries to shake down a tough, unyielding Hasidic man, only the threat of castration causes the young man to relent. Even in Tony's lithium-induced delirium, a hallucinated version of Carmela threatens castration when she learns that he has been with the voluptuous Italian woman who only exists in Tony's fantasies. At one point, Carmela wants Tony to get a vasectomy to avoid the shame of fathering a bastard child with his goomahs. Tony tells her, "Whatever's down there is God's creation."

The castrating figure that lurks in Tony's unconscious is not primarily the father he loved and admired so much. In his case the attack on his manhood and his self-esteem more likely comes from Livia, as foreshadowed in the flashback where she is wielding the fork near his eye. Mom—not Dad—is the real threat to Tony, and on some level he has always known it but has deeply repressed it. When Dr. Melfi attempts to remove the veil of repression, Tony becomes violent.

Children who are psychologically and emotionally abused by their parents must defend themselves against the realization that the parents who were supposed to protect them are actually malevolent and capricious. The children shut down the mental processes necessary for depicting thoughts and feelings both in themselves and in others so they do not have to face their parents' hostile intent, which is too overwhelming to contemplate. They must believe that their parents love them at some level because the alternative is unthinkable. For psychological development to occur, the child must make an emotional attachment to a parent or other caregiver. In abusive situations, the child is trapped in a paradox: The abuse increases the child's fear, but the fear heightens the need to attach to a parent or parental substitute in order to feel safe. To manage this situation, children must believe that somehow their mother is able to provide safety no matter how abusive she may be. Hence it is only when Tony has incontrovertible evidence that Livia has authorized the hit Uncle Junior arranged that he can fully accept that his mother is more Medea than Madonna.

For all the emphasis on patriarchy in the Mob family, Livia is clearly the power base in the Soprano family. Uncle Junior goes to her for advice on what to do when Christopher and Brendan are becoming too independent in their criminal activity. When Brendan is dispatched "Moe Green style," Christopher is spared because Livia thinks he is a good kid. Incredibly, she lays the groundwork for Uncle Junior to order a hit on her own son. First she tells him that Tony is seeing a psychiatrist. Junior is incredulous, but Livia says, "I don't want there to be any repercussions." Like a master politician, she speaks indirectly so that she will ultimately have plausible deniability if someone tries to link her to the hit. She tells Junior that Tony has private meetings with New York Mob bosses and even speculates that they might be talking about Junior. Junior responds that they must be making an end run around him and he has to act because he's the boss. Livia does not disagree.

When the botched hit is discussed on the television news, Livia is dumbfounded: "How could this happen?" Junior, dependent on Livia for his next move, asks her what they should do next. Livia responds with a clear course of action: "We go see him—he's my only son."

When Livia and Junior come to visit Tony, however, Livia appears to have a sudden onset of a dementia so severe she cannot recognize her own granddaughter. Carmela is not fooled. Ever since Carmela's wedding day, when Livia told Tony it was a mistake and that he would get bored with Carmela, she has been fully aware of her mother-in-law's ruthlessness. Carmela even confronts Livia, telling her that she uses her power "like a pro." She goes on to tell Livia that she manipulates Tony. Ever the victim, Livia responds by saying, "Wait until *you're* abandoned." When Tony tells Livia that Junior is making bad decisions, she says, "Why are you telling me? Tell Junior." Tony suggests that Livia has Junior's ear, but she says she does not want to get involved.

Because of Livia's manipulativeness, Dr. Melfi tells Tony that his mother probably has a borderline personality disorder. This diagnosis might actually be charitable because Livia is much closer to being a true psychopath than Tony. Whereas Carmela has discerned Livia's true colors, Tony has seen, but not seen, his mother's malevolence. In the culture in which he was raised, no man allows even a hint of disrespect for his mother. She is the Madonna. On the street, a negative comment about anyone's mother leads directly to a fight. After spending his adult life following his culture's mandate to love and respect his mother, Tony finally wakes up when he realizes that Livia tried to have him, her only son, killed. He has been haunted by the memory of his mother's threat to smother the kids if his father Johnny moved the family to Las

Vegas, so he plans to retaliate in kind. He goes to the hospital, intending to smother her with a pillow, but she is whisked out on a gurney in the nick of time. He realizes that she is laughing at him, and he is overcome with murderous impulses toward her. Soon he is announcing that she is dead to him.

There is little doubt that Nancy Marchand's extraordinary performance adds immeasurably to the convincingly evil core of Livia's character. David Chase says that Livia was the most difficult part to cast. He auditioned two hundred actresses before he found Marchand. Like Lorraine Bracco, Marchand was cast against type. A well-established actress, she had played a string of upper-class, Upper East Side roles, and she surprised everyone with her dead-on portrait of a New Jersey Mob momma.

Chase has openly acknowledged that Livia was based on characteristics of his own mother. Although Mother Chase never sought to exterminate her son, she was relentlessly "negative and downbeat." She was good at inducing guilt, and, like Livia, she hated the idea of going to a retirement home. Chase said that when his wife finally saw *The Sopranos*, she was struck by how much Livia was like her mother-in-law. In fact, some of Livia's dialogue came directly from the mouth of Chase's mother. His mother never used names when referring to family members. Like Livia, she referred to people by their roles—"mother-in-law," "wife," etc. She was also inclined to say, "I wish the Lord would take me" and "Oh, poor you." When Chase was seven years old, his family was cooped up in their home during a snowstorm. He kept nagging his mother to get him a Hammond organ until finally she threatened to put his eye out with a fork.

Psychotherapists are accustomed to hearing about childhood fears of maternal attacks. In an interview about how *The Sopranos* has affected society, David Chase, with tongue only partly in cheek, noted that "psychiatrists say they've got more men coming in. A surprising number of people seem to remember that their mother had tried to kill them."

Livia is the evil *magna mater* who makes Tony's criminal behavior understandable. (Livia is also the name of the scheming, ruthless wife of Augustus Caesar in Robert Graves's novels about the emperor Claudius. *I, Claudius,* the BBC miniseries based on those novels, has much of the same fascination as *The Sopranos.*) Dr. Melfi vacillates between empathizing with Tony because of the proverbial "bad mother" he has tolerated all his life and recognizing that Tony has indeed turned into his mother. The audience's response parallels Dr. Melfi's, and the fact that Tony can remain a sympathetic character in spite of his behavior is directly linked to the evil of satanic dimensions in the heart of Livia. We are amazed that Tony turned out as well as he did considering that he started life with Livia. Without much of a role model, he has tried his best to give his children a better childhood than he had. Compared to Livia, he seems almost saintly.

Like Medea, Livia is resourceful. Medea helped Jason secure the Golden Fleece. Jason later abandoned her to pursue his infatuation with the Corinthian Princess Creusa, and, as revenge, Medea killed her own and Jason's sons. She went on the lam to Athens, where she married Aegeus and later tried to make her husband poison his son. Like Medea, Livia always seems to land on her feet. Her brother-in-law Junior says of her, "If she fell into a sewer pipe, she'd come up holding a gold watch in each hand."

After her daughter Janice, comes to town, Livia tries to play one family member against the other. She calls Carmela to persuade her that Janice is up to no good—which happens to be true. After Janice shoots her fiancé, Richie Aprile, Tony comes to Livia's home to pick up Janice and take her to the bus stop. They fabricate a story about how Richie has disappeared. Livia's response is, "Oh, sure. He probably jilted her—that's the story of her life."

Tony explodes at her, "What kind of a fuckin' chance did she have with *you* as her mother? You were always naggin' her about her weight. She'd go out on a date and come home. You'd call her a fuckin' tramp."

Livia looks Tony in the eye and says, "I never said anything of the kind." Tony confronts her: "I heard you." Livia protests, "You make things up. You tell me, you tell me when I ever did anything to any of you." Tony is incredulous: "You don't know, do you? You don't have a fuckin' clue."

Livia pulls for sympathy by acknowledging her imperfections, but she also stresses that "Babies are like animals. They're no different than dogs. Somebody has to teach 'em right from wrong." She closes her diatribe with a classic maternal guilt trip: "I suppose now you're not going to kiss me. You're cruel. That's what you are."

Tony gives up, uttering, "Fuck this!" as he walks out the door and down the front steps. He is so agitated, though, that he trips and falls as he steps off the porch. He turns around and looks at Livia. Marchand, in an acting tour de force, goes from exaggerated sobbing to a smile of triumphant glee at Tony's fall and back to her sobs without missing a beat.

Also like Medea, Livia is something of a sorceress. Not only does she capture the devotion of Uncle Junior, but she has also cowed Tony into thinking that he is an ungrateful son who should berate himself for hating her. Livia exploits the cultural imperative that a boy must be a faithful son to his mother. Even after he knows that she wanted him whacked, Tony is still tormented with guilt after her death. In a moving therapy session after he learns of her death, Tony tells Dr. Melfi that he's glad she's dead, adding that he actually wished she'd die because she might have testified against him in the upcoming court case. Dr. Melfi, once again encouraging him to express his anger toward his mother, asks him how he feels about the fact that his own mother would testify against him.

Tony is emphatic: "That's a fuckin' miserable disgusting thing to be a bad son. You know, you're right. Why the fuck should I be a good son to that fuckin' demented old bat? That fuckin' selfish, miserable cunt. She ruined my father's life."

At this point, Tony has been able to articulate his rage, but Jennifer notices that he's shifting the impact of Livia's cruelty onto his father rather than himself. So she asks, "But he wasn't her son. What did she do to you?"

Tony demurs, "Come on, that's a matter of public record in here. We both know."

Tony suggests that Livia probably didn't even know what she was doing. Jennifer confronts Tony for letting his mother off. Tony tries one more tack. "Uncle denies it, you know. That she took part."

Jennifer points out that Tony's uncle loves him. She then gives him a mini-lecture in which she points out that it's common for grown children to harbor a secret wish that an aged parent would die, especially when the parent has lost all capacity for joy.

Tony is silent for a while. When he speaks, he says, "So we're probably done here, right? She's dead."

At some level Tony continues to view Livia as responsible for his problems. Her death should be liberating to him, but he can't get beyond his guilt and his persistent doubts that maybe he didn't really see what he saw when he looked at his mother. What Dr. Melfi didn't say in her sermonette is that the wish for an aging parent to die is simply a later version of murderous wishes from childhood. These feelings are fraught with guilt because your mother brought you into the world. She made your life possible. We have sympathy for Tony because we all have harbored feelings of hatred for a parent at one time or another, and like Tony, we have tried to avoid those feelings. We actually admire Tony for his efforts to be a good son despite all that Livia has done to make his life miserable.

Although Freud's original formulation of the Oedipus complex stressed how the male child wishes his father dead so he can have his mother to himself, analysts have long recognized that there is a *negative* Oedipus complex that may be just as powerful. In other words, the male child also may harbor death wishes toward his mother because he sees her as taking his father away from him. Livia is the parent who failed to affirm Tony's masculinity and psychologically castrated him by ridiculing him mercilessly, even when he is a middle-aged man who trips on the steps. Tony's murderous wishes are much more intense toward his mother than his father.

The Sopranos series is rife with empty rituals—confirmation receptions, engagement parties and, most of all, funerals. Livia's death presents the writers with a marvelous opportunity to spoof the typical reception by creating one in which everyone is delighted that the deceased is gone. The emptiness of the ritual is apparent to everyone, even Tony. He sees Meadow greeting people as they come into the house, and he says to Carmela, "Look at her, she's already becoming a robot like the rest of us. Her innocence is gone."

One of the most amusing sequences in the series occurs at the reception after Livia's funeral. Janice asks everyone to share a remembrance and begins by playing Livia's favorite song, "If I Loved You," from the musical *Carousel*. The irony of this choice is not lost on the family—no one felt loved by Livia and no one particularly loved her. When it is time to share remembrances, the silence is deadly. Hesh finally fumbles for words and comes up with the following reminiscence: "What struck me most is, she didn't mince words. Between brain and mouth, there was no interlocutor."

When it becomes Janice's turn, she tries to make lemon meringue out of a lemon: "When I was a child, my mother didn't let me rest on those laurels. She didn't flatter me. She believed that flowers blossom best among the rocks. Little water. She was tough, but she was right. And she's the reason I make videos today. Tony? Maybe you'd like to tell them how Ma saved all your childhood schoolwork and varsity letters but none of mine or Barbara's."

In response, Tony deadpans: "You just did! Wrap it up, Janice."

Christopher, who has had to snort coke and inhale enough marijuana to make his buoyancy rival that of the Goodyear blimp just to get through the funeral service, then rambles incoherently as the guests listen with perplexed looks on their faces.

Carmela decides to cut through the pretense by pointing out the pervasive hypocrisy in the room: "This is such a crock of shit! I'm sitting here thinkin' I should protect my children from the truth about their grandmother, on the one hand. On the other, I'm sayin' to myself, what kind of example am I setting? Evading and smiling, passing out Cheese Puffs, over a woman that we all know was terribly dysfunctional, who spread no cheer at all."

Carmela's mother is shocked by her breech of protocol and implores her daughter to be quiet, but Carmela is undaunted. When her mom threatens to leave, Carmela's dad waxes eloquent: "Let her talk, God damn it! We suffered for years under the yoke of that woman! Years! She estranged us from our own daughter, ruined I don't know how many goddam Christmases. I don't want to even begin to count."

The look on the guests' faces has now changed from bewilderment to horror. Speaking the truth at such functions is simply unacceptable. Carmela muses out loud, "From beyond the grave even." Carmela is prophetic. Indeed, Livia will continue to haunt Tony from beyond the grave. The night after the funeral reception, he watches a video of his favorite Cagney movie, *The Public Enemy*. As Cagney lies in bed in the hospital, his mother comes to his bedside and tells him, "You're my baby. You're going to get well and strong. All of us together again," and breaks down in tears. Then we see Cagney's corpse delivered through the front door as his mother sings while making the bed upstairs. Tears flow from Tony's eyes.

Livia is dead, but Tony hangs on to the hope that somewhere out there is a new version of his mother that is more like Jimmy Cagney's mother in *The Public Enemy*. At the same time, he mourns the loss of a fantasy that as long as his mother was alive, she might somehow be transformed into the mother he always wanted. The writers of *The Sopranos* are challenged by the absence of Tony's father as a flesh-and-blood character in the present. In an interview, David Chase expressed this concern: "We don't want to have a Mob boss who's haunted by his mother all the time. . . . You don't want him to be too much of a mama's boy."

We get to know Tony's father through a series of flashbacks. We see that Johnny Boy is a gregarious, impulsive high roller who was constantly on the move. Tony regarded him with awe and admiration, but from a distance. Johnny Boy did not make a great deal of time for father–son interaction, just as Tony does not place spending time with A.J. on the top of his priority list.

In one flashback Tony watches on a street corner as his father beats the hell out of a man who owes him money. In another, Johnny Boy takes little Janice, who regards herself as "daddy's girl," to an amusement park while Tony is left behind.

In the most revealing flashback of all, triggered by a taste of "gabagool," Tony recalls a memory of going with his dad to Satriale's Pork Store. His father tells him to wait in the car, but Tony comes inside and watches while his dad beats up Mr. Satriale for not having the money he owes him. The butcher pleads for mercy and offers to give him $30 worth of meat, but Johnny Boy is merciless and uses a meat cleaver to cut off the butcher's pinkie. Recalling this scene in therapy, Tony tells Dr. Melfi that it was not particularly trau-matic: "It was a rush."

Returning to the memory, Johnny Boy sits Tony down with him and gives him his version of the facts of life. He knows that Tony witnessed his brutality, so he instills the Soprano moral code in his son: "What you seen today is a very sad thing. You disobeyed your old man, and I oughta give the belt. But I gotta say it. A lot of boys your age would have run like a little girl, but you stayed. I know you like Mr. Satriale. We all do. He's a lovely man. The man's a gambler. He got over his head in debt. He owed me money, and he refused to pay. He avoided me. That's why you should never gamble, Anthony. What was I supposed to do? That's my livelihood. That's how I put food on the table. You should never gamble, Anthony. Let this be a lesson to you. A man honors his debts."

The moral code is clear. If someone owes you money and doesn't pay, you're justified in removing selected parts of his anatomy. It is a matter of principle, of honor. Gamblers deserve what they get. One can see the foreshadowing of Tony's treatment of Davie Scatano (Robert Patrick) a genera-tion later.

We also see one determinant of Tony's vertical split. His father is teaching him how one rationalizes the violent behav-ior as a matter of doing what's right. This lesson helps mini-mize the potential conflict between the two disparate aspects of Tony's psyche. In her own way Livia also encourages this kind of compartmentalization. Livia never actually says, "Let's kill my son." When she is confronted with the fact, she is adamant in her denial and flabbergasted that anyone would have thought that she could imagine such a thing.

Tony's memory continues as he recounts this series of events to Dr. Melfi. He sees his dad hugging his mother from behind as they sit down at the dinner table with one of Mr. Satriale's succulent roasts. As Johnny Boy hugs Livia, he sings "All of me. Why not take all of me?" in his most seductive voice. As he dances with her, he intones, "The lady loves her meat." Johnny Boy then cuts the roast, and Tony has his first fainting episode. In her therapeutic work with the memory, Jennifer emphasizes the pleasure that Livia took in having the meat brought to her. Tony acknowledged it was the only time that she seemed happy or in a good mood, and he suggested as well, "Probably the only time the Old Man got laid."

Jennifer goes on to help him see how this memory shaped his anxieties and contributed to the panic attacks: "Witnessing not only your mother's and father's sexuality but also the violence and blood so closely connected to the food you were about to eat. And also, the thought that some day you might be called upon to bring home the bacon. Like your father."

Here Dr. Melfi and the writers are sounding more Freudian than Freud. Dr. Melfi suggests that Tony has experienced a "primal scene" trauma, with all of its implications. In psychoanalytic theory, the primal scene refers to both the reality of witnessing parental intercourse and the fantasy about parental sexuality without actually observing it. The primal scene evokes feelings of rejection and exclusion, and it also raises questions in a child's mind about who's doing what to whom and why. Many children observing parental intercourse or hearing the sounds connected with sex through the bedroom walls assume that violence is involved. Hence the primal scene is often connected to violent fantasies in the child's mind. In connecting the blood and violence with the sexualization of Johnny Boy and Livia's dance in the kitchen, Dr. Melfi is helping Tony see why he might pass out rather than fully appreciate the implications of what he is observing and thinking. Later, Tony learns from Hesh that Johnny Boy suffered from the same condition. Like father, like son.

Another aspect of the "primal scene" and its presumed impact on the child is that it makes the child recognize that his mother's thoughts aren't exclusively focused on him. She has private experiences and thoughts related to an independent and separate relationship with his father that excludes him. Tony's sense of himself as an outsider, as someone who is always in the role of onlooker, is powerfully reinforced by the flashbacks, all of which show him viewing events that he is not supposed to see: his father cutting off Mr. Satriale's finger, his father and Janice going to the amusement park where Johnny Boy will do some of his dirty work with fellow thugs and, of course, the sexual overtures of Johnny Boy to Livia. As an adult, he attempts to play golf with his upper-middle-class neighbors and feels like a "dancing bear" on display because he does not fit in. We can speculate that his emphasis on absolute loyalty, his Mob "family" and his need for belonging are all defensive strategies that help him undo that sense of isolation and exclusion from his childhood.

Because Johnny Boy died of lung cancer when Tony was a young man, the audience sees Tony as a man without a paternal role model. Uncle Junior, who is always shadowing Johnny Boy in the flashbacks, serves as a less than ideal surrogate father. His bond with Livia suggests that he has dutifully replaced his deceased brother by devoting himself to Livia and looking after her needs. However, just as Laius tried to destroy his son in the Oedipus myth, Uncle Junior tries to eliminate his surrogate son by ordering a hit on him. Junior is deeply troubled by this decision, however, and spends the morning puking up his guts when Tony is supposed to be killed. Livia, on the other hand, appears unfazed.

Tony and Uncle Junior are locked in a power struggle for control of the Mob family. Tony shrewdly defers to Junior's leadership while working behind the scenes to control the operations to his advantage. As the series develops, Uncle Junior is shown progressively deteriorating and consigned to a fate of house arrest where he watches soap operas and gets his hand stuck in the garbage disposal.

Uncle Junior is not the lion king that his brother was. He played by the rules and avoided ruffling feathers. As a member of the royal family, he gained everyone's respect by proxy and moved up the hierarchy as a birthright—*not* by establishing his authority through testosterone-crazed acts of bravery.

Uncle Junior appears to lack the stomach for Mob life. He has three strikes against him: 1) he seeks advice from women; 2) he "eats sushi" (performs cunnilingus); and 3) he tosses his cookies when he has to order a hit. He can't seem to make a correct move on his own and always needs the guidance of others to point him in the right direction. On top of everything, he is superstitious and constantly worries about his health because cancer deaths "come in threes."

In many families uncles occupy a special niche in the lives of their nieces and nephews. The term *avuncular,* which literally means pertaining to an uncle, with its connotations of kindliness, captures the quality of that role. The uncle is a wise, often funny, stand-in for the father, who circles in an orbit outside the conflict-ridden relationship of parent and child. His "once-removed" status allows him to dispense advice and affection from a position unfettered by the intensity of the niece or nephew's nuclear family relationships. But Junior comes from a different mold. Hence Tony is even deprived of the uncle-nephew relationship that so many of us cherish. Like Claudius in *Hamlet,* Uncle Junior moves in on Livia after the death of his brother and, in his platonic way, relates to her as though she is his wife. Tony, like Hamlet, deeply resents him for taking that position with his mother. Junior, on the other hand, redirects any rivalry with his brother that he may have once had toward his nephew.

Whenever Tony and Junior meet, however, the contempt between them is palpable. Tony visits Uncle Junior in prison, and Junior swears that Livia had nothing to do with ordering the hit. Tony asserts that Livia is dead to him, but Junior insists that he needs to make peace with her. Tony recognizes that there is an advantage in having Junior regarded as head of the family; namely, there is less heat on him. Junior, on the other hand, is not a fan of Tony, but he, too, is careful to discern which way the wind is blowing. When Richie Aprile comes to Junior dripping with obsequiousness and informing Junior that Tony is screwing him over, Junior is appreciative, and he encourages Richie to develop an alliance against Tony. He kisses Richie and tells him that he's "a good boy."

Later, however, Richie comes back empty-handed, indicating that he could not gain the confidence of other made men to join him in his plan to eliminate Tony. Junior reflects on Richie's lack of salesmanship. He tells his goombah Bobby that Richie is a loser and resigns himself to the fact that Richie is not respected. He is better off with Tony, so he informs Tony that Richie is making a move against him. Before Tony can bump off Richie, though, his sister beats him to it.

Junior has lived a long life by staying in the good graces of the movers and shakers. Tony cannot trust him to play the role of father, so despite Junior's presence, Tony is essentially orphaned. Part of the poignancy stirred by Tony's character is that he is essentially both fatherless and motherless, an orphan.

Tony is clearly no match for Livia. To find such a match, we need look no further than Tony's next of kin, Janice. Certain to be a unanimous pick for the Psychopath Hall of Fame, Janice is, as Livia puts it, "a snake in the grass." She has spent most of her adult life searching for spiritual enlightenment and government handouts. She arrives from the state of Washington, where she has been on total disability. She announces that she has changed her name to "Parvati Wasatch." Parvati was the consort of Lord Shiva and is known for loyalty, obedience and devotion to one's elders. She would love to be a solid citizen, of course, but the old carpal tunnel syndrome is just too much for her to bear.

Ever the devoted daughter, Janice ministers to Livia and visits her in her hospital room. Out of profound compassion for her mother and an intense interest in positioning herself as the next tenant of Livia's house, she strongly encourages Tony to authorize a DNR (do not resuscitate) order in case poor Livia should have a cardiac arrest in the hospital. Tony, who has power of attorney, does not want to bother with it.

Janice, whose compassion for her mother knows no bounds, is not deterred by Tony's reluctance, and she manages to think of other ways that Livia might be put out of her misery. During one conversation when Janice visits Livia in the hospital, her eyes are distracted by a poster on the wall showing a staircase to be used for rapid exit in case of a fire. Throughout her conversation with Livia, her face is adorned with sugary sweet smiles as she talks about taking Livia home and being her nursemaid. Her mind is preoccupied, though, with images of her mother falling down the stairs. She just can't seem to get her mind off that image. Janice reminds one of the observation once made by Hamlet about his uncle, Claudius:

> *Oh villain, villain, smiling, damned villain!*
> *My tables,—meet it is I set it down,*
> *That one may smile, and smile, and be a villain.*

Meanwhile, Janice meets up with Richie Aprile and cements their romantic relationship by submitting to sex at gunpoint. She assures her sister-in-law Carmela that such behavior is no different than wearing a nurse's uniform, and keeps him from straying to prostitutes, who have too much dignity to play such games.

She also incites Richie to challenge her brother Tony for leadership of the Mob. When Tony presents Richie, fresh out of prison, with $50,000 to get him started, Janice deprecates Tony's generosity by saying her dad gave the same get-out-of-jail bonus thirty years ago. She suggests that a half a million would be a more appropriate amount, given inflation and cost-of-living increases.

Uncle Junior is onto Janice and recalls how she stole money from his wallet when she was just a kid. When he reveals to Tony that Richie is going to make a move on him, he says in passing, "You gotta wonder what role Janice is playin' in all this."

Sibling rivalry does not end with the passage into adulthood. I once saw a fifty-three-year-old man in therapy who gave me a running commentary on his older sister's successes. I heard about her new cars, her boats, her homes, and even where she went on her vacations. My patient tormented himself by comparing his own accomplishments and acquisitions to hers. If she got a Saab, he felt he had to buy a Mercedes. If she went to Paris, he would arrange a trip to Bali. Although he joked about their competition, he was obsessed to the point where his only pleasure was outdoing his sister. I had no doubt that if she walked by a staircase, he would do his best to trip her. Brothers and sisters often are convinced that a sibling's success reflects badly on them. This type of rivalry reminds one of the theological definition of envy—joy at others' misfortune, despair at others' success.

Janice's romantic relationships are in greater jeopardy when Janice is holding the gun rather than having it pointed at her head. She dispatches Richie after he makes the mistake of hitting her in the mouth. A touching moment passes between Tony and Janice when he takes her to the bus station to tell her good-bye. Tony says that it was "a pretty good visit," but Janice won't buy into the pretense. She asks, "What's wrong with our family?" Tony tells her he sees a psychiatrist who says that Livia is a narcissistic personality, that she's not capable of experiencing joy. Tony adds ruefully, "Dad—all he did was experience joy."

They hug good-bye, and Tony suggests that she should go back into therapy.

After Livia passes away, Tony calls Janice to scream at her for not returning from Washington to attend the funeral. She is living with a 19-year-old fiancé, who she says can "go all night," and as usual, she is penniless. On the phone, however, she tells Tony that the reason she can't come is that she has good reasons for not setting foot in New Jersey. Tony reassures her that "the case is colder than your tits." Finally, the conversation gets around to the real problem, which is that she cannot afford the ticket. When Tony offers to buy her a plane ticket, Janice is calm and calculating. Could he also pay for her fiancé's ticket? She also wants an update about what is being said about Richie's disappearance. Her own hide is of much more concern to her than her mother's death.

The similarities between Janice and Livia jump off the screen at the viewer. She has borrowed her mother's scheming and manipulative modus operandi. And despite Tony's loathing for Janice, she manages to ensnare him by invoking family loyalty in the same way that Livia does. Tony feels there is a cultural imperative to come to the aid of his sister, even though he hates her. He knows she provoked the beating by the Russian thugs, but he might seem weak if he did nothing in response to an assault on a blood relative. Like it or not, Tony is the "go-to guy" when family problems occur. Janice uses him to accomplish her own ends, and like a good psychopath, she is utterly without remorse. She is, in the final analysis, her mother's daughter.

SCENES FROM A MARRIAGE: GODFATHER KNOWS BEST

Folk wisdom has it that men pick women like their mothers to marry. There is some truth to this, but selecting a mate is more complicated than the old saying implies. We grow up embroiled in a set of conflicts with each of our parents. We choose a partner with the conscious hope that the pain stemming from those conflicts can be healed. A man who grew up with a mother who rarely hugged or kissed him may choose a wife who is effusive in showing her love for him. A woman whose father was always on the road and never had time for her may pick a husband who likes to stay at home and tend the garden. However, change is not always welcomed, and we may secretly be ambivalent about giving up the old patterns we learned in childhood. Mate selection involves two wishes that are in conflict with each other: the wish to re-create the childhood attachment to the parent and the wish to find a new relationship that will heal the wounds from the parent–child conflict. Hence a man may choose a woman who holds out the promise of providing a different experience for him while also assuring that the relationship with his mother will be repeated. This is certainly true of Tony's choice of Carmela.

The reader may think I'm way off base here. Carmela? A junior Livia? Nonsense! Even the local expert on the Soprano family, Dr. Jennifer Melfi, calls Carmela "the one good decision" Tony ever made about women. And Carmela is indisputably the most sympathetic character in the series. The long-suffering, martyred wife, she puts up with Tony's philandering, his tirades against her and the children, his secretiveness about his criminal activities and his preference for hanging out with the boys. Even though she has a wealth of material pleasures, Carmela lives a life of isolation, and the audience can't help feeling sorry for her.

Not only is she victimized by Tony's shenanigans, but when she seeks solace from the priest, Father Phil, she merely trades one corrupt man for another. One of the funniest and most touching subplots in *The Sopranos* is Carmela's attachment to Father Phil. Like Tony, Father Phil has an inner schism, in his case between the sanctimonious and the lustful. He visits Carmela's house while Tony is off with Meadow garroting snitches and schmoozing with college admissions officers. Father Phil tells Carmela that he has a "Jones for her ziti." When he makes a fire in the fireplace, Carmela tells him that Tony never does that for her. She tearfully confides in Father Phil that Tony must have concealed the gender of his therapist because he is having sex with her.

Father Phil presents a stark contrast to Dr. Melfi. He, too, is a "helping professional" who is ministering to Carmela in the way that Dr. Melfi ministers to Tony. He hears confession from her in her home while the two of them are watching a video of *The Remains of the Day* (1993) a Masterpiece Theatre knockoff about a celibate relationship between a passionate woman and an incorruptible servant. Carmela confesses that she wanted things for the kids and for herself, so she went along with her husband's criminal activity. Now she worries about God's wrath for colluding with Tony's corruption.

Compared with Dr. Melfi, Father Phil has poor professional boundaries. He exploits and manipulates Carmela's longings for him. He gets her to cook for him. After he gives her communion in her living room, he hugs her tightly. They eventually fall asleep on the couch with her head on his shoulder. Father Phil looks at Carmela romantically after a phone call wakes them up, and just as he's about to kiss her, he dashes to the toilet to relieve himself of his stomach contents and his guilt. The morning after, Father Phil, bleary-eyed and hung over, confesses to Carmela that he lusts in his heart. He says the previous night was one of the most difficult tests that

God has ever given him. Carmela is swept off her feet by him but laments her fate of finding one of the few straight priests in New Jersey.

Carmela may be victimized, but she is not a mean-spirited voice of doom like her mother-in-law. She finally wises up to Father Phil and realizes that he is actually Tony Soprano in a clerical collar. She dismisses him: "You like the whiff of sexuality that never goes anyplace." She tells him that he manipulates sexually thirsty women and that it's all tied in with food. Phil leaves the Soprano household with his tail between his legs, knowing that he has been emotionally "whacked."

The fact that Carmela is exploited by not one but two men deeply distresses the audience, who think of Carmela as the voice of conscience in the Soprano family. Not only does she confront her priest, but she also has the guts to talk back to Livia; no one else in the family demonstrates this kind of courage. She bluntly tells Livia that her manipulative style is "This poor-mother-nobody-cares-about-me victim crap" and that she uses her power "like a pro."

Carmela can't even find comfort in her own daughter, who refuses to take their annual mother–daughter trip to the Plaza. Spurned by an ungrateful daughter, exploited by a mooching priest, undermined by a ruthless mother-in-law and cheated on by a philandering husband, Carmela is thrilled to get an invitation to have lunch with the dean at Columbia. He appears to care about her daughter's progress in college, but the real nature of his interest is clear when he asks Carmela for a $50,000 donation. Dean Ross (Frank Wood) confides to Carmela that he is actually second-generation Italian American, and his name used to be Rossi. Meadow's reaction to the lunch with the dean is succinct: "How corrupt!" Tony refers to the meeting as a "shakedown." One can only wonder if it is a coincidence that the dean's original last name is the same as that of Dr. Melfi's rapist.

So far this description of Carmela makes her seem quite different from Livia, who is more tormentor than tormented. Do Tony and Carmela really fit the model of a husband who marries a woman who will assure that his experience with his mother will be repeated? The answer is straightforward—yes and no. She is both different from her mother-in-law and similar to her. Like the rest of us, Tony is attracted to the surface characteristics of Carmela. She is nurturing, attractive and dependable. But there is a bully-in-waiting just under the surface that resonates with his experience of Livia. The writers of *The Sopranos* are far too sophisticated to divide the world into victims and victimizers.

Carmela's dark side is detected by the radar of Dr. Krakower (Sully Boyar), a senior psychiatrist recommended to Carmela by Dr. Melfi, who had been his student. In this highly unconventional psychiatric consultation, Dr. Krakower forces her to face her active role in the corruption around her. Carmela tells her psychiatrist that she feels her husband is a good man and a good father. Dr. Krakower is unconvinced: "You tell me he's a depressed criminal, prone to anger, sexually unfaithful. Is that your definition of a good man?"

Carmela, Krakower suggests, is nothing less than Tony's accomplice. Carmela argues that all she does is make his dinner and wash his clothes. Dr. Krakower retorts that "enabler" might be a more precise job description than accomplice. He then says that Tony should read Dostoevsky's *Crime and Punishment* and reflect on his crimes for seven years in a jail cell. Only then might he be redeemed. The session ends when Krakower informs Carmela that there is no charge because he won't take "blood money." He also cautions her, "One thing you can never say is that you haven't been told."

Dr. Krakower's jarring technique is a sharp counterpoint to Jennifer Melfi's efforts to form a therapeutic alliance with Tony and help him understand the origins of his antisocial behavior. Whereas Dr. Melfi's ex-husband Richard accuses her of "cheesy moral relativism," Dr. Krakower might well be charged with "cheesy relative moralizing." His approach drew a variety of responses from the *Slate* analysts. One suggested that even though he moved too rapidly and completely ignored Carmela's defenses, "He lets us know that this is his technique, and it may be called for in this situation." Another pundit argues that Krakower's forthright confrontation of Carmela's collusion in corruption was a way of getting rid of the patient: "As analysts, we always have to reflect upon the meaning of starting a treatment with telling a patient how she must live her life and also laying out that they can expect no help from us for anything short of following through on our expectation." Margaret Crastnopol, the only female analyst in the *Slate* group, sees the introduction of Krakower as an example of subtle sexism in the writing of *The Sopranos*:

> As a potential solution, the senior therapist character is made to be the one who can make the moral judgment, name names as it were, prescribe "right action" for Carmela, and rescue Melfi from her clinical/countertransferential predicament all at the same time.

I find myself torn about Krakower's behavior. There is something compelling about a gutsy therapist who cuts through pretense and denial. When I was in training, a crusty, irascible supervisor of mine interviewed one of my patients in my presence. He asked the young man why he wasn't working. My patient offered a long-winded explanation, replete with myriad excuses for his unemployment. When he finished his rant, my supervisor looked at him squarely and said, "Sounds to me like you're a lazy bum." I cringed and waited for my patient to explode in anger. After a brief silence, the young man responded, "No sir, I am not." My supervisor was unfazed: "Then prove it," he said. The interview ended, and I tried to patch up the damage by explaining to my patient that my supervisor was just being provocative. (I was secretly beginning to wonder if I should have specialized in ophthalmology.) But something happened during that interview, and my patient had a job two weeks later.

One has to question whether Dr. Krakower's message can get across if there is no effort at empathic understanding and the building of a trusting relationship. Some patients would be so hurt by his confrontation that they would ignore any advice he dispensed. In a sea of moral relativism, though, where deans and priests and therapists seem as slippery as loan sharks, a straight shooter like Krakower is a welcome addition to the cast of characters. One also can speculate about Dr. Melfi's motivation in referring Carmela to Dr. Krakower. He'd been her teacher, so she must have known that he would take a hard-line approach. She may even have guessed that Dr. Krakower would encourage Carmela to leave Tony. Was she unconsciously setting things up so that Dr. Krakower would dispose of a rival? Or was she recognizing that Carmela had been "charmed by a sociopath" in the same way that she had and was hoping that Dr. Krakower would talk some sense into her? Or both?

How the writers created the dialogue for the meeting with Dr. Krakower is fascinating. Ronald Green, a professor of psychiatry at Dartmouth School of Medicine, serves as an informal psychiatric consultant to his sister, Robin Green, one of the team of five writers. He once read *Crime and Punishment* while recovering from an illness. Shortly thereafter, he saw two patients in succession who had molested their own children. Green told them they had sentenced their children to decades of suffering. He suggested they read Dostoevsky's magnum opus because the author suggests redemption is possible through suffering, even for a murderer. He remembered Raskolnikov's sentence—seven years of chopping rocks in the Gulag. Green then advised the patients that after they finish the novel, they should turn themselves in and arrange severe punishment. The pain they would suffer might teach them something about the pain they had inflicted on their children. If they still wanted therapy afterward, they could return. Both men left angry.

Carmela's encounter with Dr. Krakower makes it clear she is not simply a victim. She doesn't like what she hears from him, so she turns to the confessional with Father Obosi (Isaach De Bankole), an African priest training to be a psychologist. He suggests they move from the confessional to his office, where he tells her that God understands that we all live "in the middle of tensions." He suggests that she "learn to live in the good part."

Carmela likes this version of therapy better. She knows she is complicit with Tony's criminality, but she is too invested in the material advantages to give up what she has. She helps him hide bundles of cash and weapons in the house when they are tipped off about an FBI raid. When she needs to get a letter of recommendation for Meadow's college application to Georgetown, she demonstrates that she has studied under the tutelage of Tony Soprano. Meadow has told her it might be a "reach" for her to get into Georgetown, so Carmela asks her neighbor, Jeanie Cusemano, to ask her sister, Joan, a graduate of Georgetown Law School, to write a letter of recommendation.

Jeanie's sister refuses—she's already written letters for more deserving applicants—but Carmela is undaunted. She appears in Joan's office with a pie and a smile pasted on her face. Carmela says, "I don't think you understand. I want you to write that letter."

Carmela has mastered Tony's bullying tactics, and she uses them perfectly when she needs something for her children. Joan, it turns out, finds it prudent not to refuse Carmela. Jeanie informs Carmela that Joan was "knocked out" by Meadow's transcript and wrote the letter after all. Carmela smiles and asks if she can have a copy of the letter.

Here we see traces of Livia in Tony's choice of a mate. As much as she loathes Livia's manipulative methods, Carmela uses them to good advantage. Moreover, just as Livia was the power base in Tony's childhood, Carmela is the ultimate power in Tony's current family. She wants to give $50,000 to Columbia, but Tony insists that he won't go over $5,000. Carmela is unfazed and issues an order to Tony that is as implacable as it is despairing: "You gotta do something nice for me today." Tony capitulates because he knows the consequences for crossing Carmela. He even agrees to a vasectomy at Carmela's insistence (although she later retracts her demand). Dr. Melfi shows that she thoroughly understands

Tony when she tells him, "You'll never leave your wife. . . . Your own selfishness is too strong to let that happen."

Not surprisingly, the same forces that influence mate selection contribute to the decision to stay in a marriage. A man reaches a point where his wife has partly delivered on the promise to be different from his mother while also upholding the unconscious contract of being like his mother. At one level, he loves her for how she is different and hates her for how she is the same. At another level, he hates her for not being like his mother—"Why can't you bring me soup when I'm sick like my mom did?!" The particular mixture of hate and love that is the fundamental quality of all intimate human relationships fuels an ongoing effort to extract what he wants from his wife while he seethes with resentment at how she has disappointed him. The man feels a secret sense of triumph in not getting what he wants from his wife. He may think smugly: "See? I was right about women."

No matter how awful Livia was to Tony, she was his mother. He turned to her for protection when he felt unsafe even though she herself was the source of his fear. Painful, tormenting relationships are his terra firma. He doesn't welcome change. The intense fights with Carmela assure him that he is on the familiar territory of his childhood and spare him from a sense of being lost. And he still has moments of love with Carmela that he never had with Livia. As George Bernard Shaw observed, getting what you want may be at least as disturbing as not getting it. Marriage is always a compromise between the two.

Carmela's despair escalates in the course of the second season. She sits around the house reading *Memoirs of a Geisha* and listening to Andrea Bocelli sing "Time to Say Goodbye." Her sister-in-law Janice criticizes her for staying in her marriage and expecting so little of herself. Carmela finally hits bottom when Tony once again fails to appear at A.J.'s swim meet. She demands an explanation: "Wherever you were, it couldn't have been more important than letting your son know that you care about him." Tony is incensed: "No! Only you care. Fuck you!" Carmela heaves the nearest breakable object at Tony and screams, "No, fuck you!" Tony has to grab her arms and throw her onto the couch. Carmela could have benefited from British actress Jill Bennett's experience. About her stormy marriage to the "angry young man" of British theater John Osborne, she quipped: "Never marry a man who hates his mother because he'll end up hating you."

We can understand why Tony doesn't leave Carmela. As Dr. Melfi suggests, he's lucky to have her. But why does Carmela stay? She sees marriage as sacred, of course, but in the same way that Tony is both reestablishing his relationship with his mother and simultaneously trying to change it, Carmela is re-creating something from her childhood as well. The brief glimpses we have of Carmela's parents suggest that they too have lived lives of quiet desperation. They keep their suffering to themselves, but once in a while it bursts out, as during Livia's funeral reception. Carmela's model of marriage has been one of barely controlled hostility and long-standing resentments. Edie Falco has some ideas about her character's attachment to Tony: "There is something, I think, about his running around, his evasiveness about what he does, that provides something that she needs. If he were to suddenly become the husband she pretends to want, I don't know that it would be as fulfilling or satisfactory to her as it is right now. The complaining, the confusion, and the anger and the disappointment, I think it's a very integral part of their connection."

The actress is clearly in touch with her character's motivation and with an unassailable fact of human nature. As Dostoevsky observed, "In despair there are the most intense enjoyments." Most marriages involve some self-imposed suffering, the origins of which are externalized and blamed on the partner. Marriage is a game of grievance collection. Over time the partners feel significantly mistreated and irreparably hurt, but they are deeply committed to perpetuating the relationship as a way of providing a constant reminder to the spouse of his or her insensitivities and shortcomings. There is a peculiar kind of virtue in suffering. Partners feel entitled to a special form of recognition from each other because they have put up with so much for so long. I have often wondered if tears are shed at weddings partly because everyone—and perhaps the bride and groom themselves—knows that the ecstasy of holy matrimony will be followed by the agony of failed expectations. As Heinrich Heine noted, "The music at a wedding procession always reminds me of the music of soldiers going into battle."

Carmela was disillusioned with Tony long ago, but she won't give up the hope, which Dr. Melfi seems to share, that Tony may ultimately be redeemable, that he will be transformed from an antisocial thug into a decent family man. The culturally sanctioned idealization of mothers that causes Tony to see but not see the despicable aspects of Livia also operate in his relationship with Carmela. He puts her on a pedestal, assigning her the purified role of the mother of his children. He looks for passionate sex elsewhere—with his Russian goomahs or at the local Mercedes dealership.

The elevation of certain women to the status of "Madonna" and the denigration of a different set of women to the level of "whore" has a long history. In 1910, in a paper entitled "A Special Type of Choice of Object Made by Men," Sigmund Freud stressed that certain men must regard their mothers as individuals of unquestionable moral purity. This sanitized view of maternal sexuality leads to a man's treating one group of women as worthy of marriage but not sex and another as worthy of sex but not marriage. This internal split prevents these men from closely connecting sexual passion and romantic love. The combination of the two resonates too closely with the incestuous love for mother they experienced as children. Tony's vertical split allows him to lavish birthday gifts on Carmela and profess his love for her while shtupping goomahs on the side.

This bifurcated pattern of relating to women is not the exclusive province of gangsters. In fact, it is a common reason that men come to therapy. A high-powered executive once consulted me because his wife would not accept that he needed women on the side to satisfy sexual cravings that he would never impose on her. He insisted that he was being considerate of her by not asking her to perform oral sex. His internal division between the kind of woman you marry and the kind you seek out for sex made perfect sense to him, and he seemed genuinely surprised that she could not accept his way of thinking. He said to me with an astonished look on his face, "I don't get it. I was honest and told her everything, but she's still mad at me. Does she want me to be deceitful?"

Gloria Trillo in *The Sopranos* is the kind of woman men seek out for sex rather than marriage. Gloria is about Dr. Melfi's age, Italian-American and successful. For Tony, her position as a Mercedes seller lends her a certain panache that the Russian goomahs lack. She may act like a whore in the bedroom, but she has enough superficial class to intoxicate Tony and make her a suitable surrogate for his therapist and a counterpoint to his wife. As Ringstrom observed in our *Slate* discussions: "She is now the third woman emotionally linked to Tony who occupies the same therapeutic office space—Dr. Melfi's office. All three women's psyches converge there and now must confront the fact that each of them in their own highly private ways has a powerful attraction to and agenda for Tony Soprano. Just as important is that on some level he knows this, too."

Gloria has the passion that Tony longs to see in Dr. Melfi or Carmela, but her sexual intensity comes with a price. Eavesdropping on one of her therapy sessions, we learn that she tried to kill herself after her last boyfriend jilted her. This morsel of history is a classic symptom of borderline personality disorder, which is characterized by impulsiveness, emotional instability, self-mutilation, suicide attempts in response to failed relationships, chronic emptiness, chaotic relationships, intense anger and a terror of being alone. It's no accident, of course, that Dr. Melfi applied the same diagnosis to Livia.

Borderline personality disorder is one of the thornier designations in psychiatry. We have all encountered people who fit this diagnostic category in the course of our lives. Although psychiatric diagnosis is not foremost in our minds when we break up with a loved one, the borderline characteristics often don't become evident until the threat of abandonment surfaces. My informal criteria: Anyone who can hurl a 16-ounce London broil, break a vase and scream "I hate you" within the space of ten seconds gets a big "yes" in the borderline column. Which is what Gloria does when Tony walks out on their high-fat, wild-sex dinner to tend to a crisis with his cronies.

We know about Tony's attraction to women with borderline personality disorder long before he meets Gloria. His Russian girlfriend Irina also screams "I hate you" and throws a statue against the door when Tony leaves. When Tony decides he has to end this relationship, she says, "If you go, I'll kill myself." Tony recognizes the similarity between Gloria and Irina during a therapy session. He reluctantly acknowledges that Gloria was just "another Irina with a college degree."

Like Tony's mother, Gloria loves to criticize Tony. The writers put words in Gloria's mouth that seem to come directly from Livia's lexicon: "Poor you! You got a fuckin' dream life compared to mine. No one cares if I'm alive or dead." When Tony suggests that maybe their relationship isn't working out so well, Gloria responds with a guilt trip worthy of his mother: "Fine. I'll sit back like a mute while you screw every woman out there." She accuses him of being self-absorbed and narcissistic. Yet she makes him feel like a man in her bedroom.

People who are close to those who suffer from borderline personality disorder often say they feel they're on an emotional roller coaster. The highs may be wonderful, but the lows are terrifying. The intensity of the sex may be thrilling, but the intensity of the anger is downright chilling. Many have the feeling of walking in a minefield.

When Tony is fed up with Gloria's angry and impulsive behavior and tries to get out of the relationship, Gloria reveals the classic borderline reaction to rejection. Her behavior suggests that she has modeled her life on the Glenn Close character in *Fatal Attraction*. She insinuates herself into the bosom of Tony's family. She drives Carmela home so she can pump her for information about the family, and in the throes of rage at Tony, she threatens to reveal their affair to Carmela and the children. After Tony has come close to throttling Gloria, he realizes that he is locked in a repetitive cycle of destructive relationships with women. He acknowledges in his session with Dr. Melfi that Gloria reminded him of her, and together they can trace back his longing for a different type of mothering than he received as a child—more like the hallucinated Italian woman nursing the baby than Livia threatening to poke his eye out with a fork.

Tony has used his vertical split to maintain a romanticized and idealized view of Gloria in the same way that he refused to acknowledge his mother's malevolence. His schism enables him to approach disastrous and unsuitable women with hopeful yearning that they will provide him the love and affirmation of the elusive all-giving mother. As his insight increases, however, he can acknowledge to Dr. Melfi that one minute Gloria "is fine, the next minute she's a fucking lunatic." Dr. Melfi asks a simple poignant question of Tony: "Does she seem happy to you?"

After a lifetime of self-delusion, Tony recognizes that he is driven to attach himself to women who hold out the promise of being different from his mother but who ultimately end up having far too much in common with her. This repetition compulsion, as Freud called it, has led Tony down one blind alley after another. As my *Slate* colleague Margaret Crastnopol points out, Gloria, Carmela, Meadow and Livia all lack the kind of social and economic power their men have. They create recognition for themselves through their association with men. Even Dr. Melfi finds a secret form of specialness in her role as the therapist to a mobster media celebrity. For Jennifer, Tony also represents a challenge to the legal impotence of the judicial system and an opportunity for avenging her humiliation at the hands of the rapist.

Crastnopol points out that Gloria, like Irina, holds out a promise that she may glory in Tony's potency. He learns quickly that this promise is only half the story. When the sex is over, Gloria reveals her castrating side. She humiliates Tony and deflates him in true Livia Soprano style. Gloria's admiration of him is a drug that he hopes will heal his pain and erase the haunting ghost of his mother. But Tony sees that the relationship is doomed. Like the siren song that lures Ulysses, Gloria's sales pitch on the car lot is the death rattle.

The *sturm und drang* of Tony and Carmela's marriage is gut-wrenching and difficult to watch. Fortunately, our horror is intermittently interrupted by a satiric counterpoint that is closely related to a familiar television genre—the family sitcom. In an interview Lorraine Bracco made a keen observation: "How could you not like a man who is searching to do the right thing? It's *Father Knows Best* for the millennium." Part of the black humor in *The Sopranos* stems from Tony's insistence on old-fashioned family values. When Meadow reminds him that it's the '90's, he retorts that in his home it is still 1954. He desperately wants to be Robert Young, the wise father dispensing advice to Princess, Kitten and Bud, but he can't quite pull it off. (HBO originally wanted to name the show "Family Man.")

The perils and pitfalls of parenthood unite Tony and Carmela as allies who must confront the challenges of raising Meadow and A.J. A recurrent theme in the series is the deconstruction of the mythology of power. Tony Soprano, the omnipotent boss of a New Jersey Mob family, is powerless to tame his own children.

When Tony finds Meadow wildly partying in Livia's house with her strung-out teenage friends, he takes her home and lets her know she will be facing discipline. Carmela and Tony lie in bed and contemplate their options. Carmela complains: "You're over a barrel no matter what you do. You take away her car, you become her chauffeur. You ground her, you gotta stay home weekends and be prison guards." Tony laments that they can't restrain her physically because they'll be accused of child abuse. Both parents agree they have to impose consequences if Meadow is to be reined in. But, adds Tony, conspiratorially, "Let's just not overplay our hand. 'Cuz if she finds out we're powerless, we're fucked!"

Every parent tuned into HBO reacts with a smile—if not a grimace—of recognition. Like Tony and Carmela, the Ozzie and Harriet of mobster land, we know we are powerless to change our adolescent children's behavior. All we can do is cross our fingers and pray that they make it to age twenty-one without jail sentences, drug overdoses or pregnancies. All of us grew up watching sitcoms and wondering why our families were not like the ones on television. One father of three sons whom I saw in therapy for several years confided that he modeled himself on Fred MacMurray in *My Three Sons* because he had no role models in his dysfunctional family. After suffering the slings and arrows of fatherhood, however, he resigned himself to the fact that since his three boys hadn't watched the show, they had no understanding of how they were supposed to behave.

Whereas Robert Young in *Father Knows Best* called his daughters Kitten and Princess, Tony has a more creative nickname for his daughter. The morning after the party, he asks Carmela, "Where's the Bride of Frankenstein?" When the teenage Elsa Lanchester finally descends into the kitchen, Tony and Carmela fumble to come up with appropriate punishment. Meadow rescues them by suggesting that they take away her Discover card for two weeks. Tony Soprano, New Jersey Mob boss, a master of hard-line negotiations, exercises his legendary toughness with a counteroffer: "Three." Meadow later triumphantly confides to a friend that she meted out her own punishment.

Tony's relationship with Meadow adds a poignancy to *The Sopranos* that transcends the black comedy of the show. Meadow's success may be the only genuine joy that Tony and Carmela experience. Tony has devoted his life to providing for his family so that his children can stand on his shoulders and live the American dream without resorting to crime. Meadow is bright enough to get into Columbia, beautiful enough to attract any man she wants and genuinely enamored of her dad despite his shortcomings. She is the light of Tony's life.

Tony often turns to Meadow as a confidant, particularly when he and Carmela are at odds with each other. Meadow affirms that there is something good about him when he despairs of finding affirmation from the other women in his life. She makes him feel lovable when he is filled with self-loathing. At one point, when Tony is drinking himself into oblivion at the kitchen table, he asks if she knows that he loves her. Meadow replies that she does. He tells her, "Your mother doesn't think I love you enough." Meadow responds, "And you listen to her?" Meadow becomes a conspirator, pushing away her mother and forging a father–daughter bond. She tells her father exactly what he wants to hear.

As the conversation continues, Tony, on the verge of tears, explains, "Everything I do and everything I've done and everything I will do . . . it's all for you and your buddy. You know that. . . . I mean, I tell people you're like your mother, but you're all me. Nothing gets by you. And I know you think I'm a hypocrite."

Meadow's response, "Sometimes we're all hypocrites," is music to Tony's ears. She knows he needs her forgiveness and love to make it through the night, and she provides both.

The relationship between a father and daughter is like no other. Most daughters figure out that they are the apple of their father's eye and take advantage of it anytime they can. A big strong man becomes putty in their hands. Throughout childhood, a daughter may view her mother as an obstacle to a closer relationship with Dad. Running into Dad in the middle of the night long after Mom has gone to sleep may be a special moment for a daughter. Fathers often treat their daughters differently when the two of them are alone. The conversation can be more candid when Mom is not listening. Secrets are passed and kept. Knowing winks in Mom's presence are later used as signals of the shared knowledge.

Meadow's ability to negotiate life successfully offers Tony some form of redemption. She will live the life that he couldn't lead. She will be the embodiment of that kernel of goodness within Tony that gets buried beneath his ruthlessness. Indeed, Meadow serves a special function for Tony—an extension of his idealized version of himself, the fantasy of being a solid citizen in the upper-middle class of New Jersey with a family he can be proud of.

To protect his vision of who Meadow should become, Tony plays the vicious racist and anti-Semitic card. He confronts Meadow's African-American/Jewish boyfriend and warns him that he has business associates who are black who don't want his son with their daughters, and he adds ominously, "I don't want their sons with mine." Meadow's relationship with Noah is now in serious jeopardy, as is her bond with Tony. Carmela is sensitive to the damage. She confronts Tony and tries to soothe Meadow, explaining that Tony "comes from a place and a time where he thinks he has your best interests at heart." Meadow is unmoved: "New Jersey? The third millennium?"

The love of parents for a teenage daughter is inevitably contaminated by a particular vision of what that daughter should become. A script has been written, and the blossoming young woman is the central character. The narrative of this drama is almost always a variation on the parents' own fantasies of what they wished they had become. Sometimes the script is explicit. Other times the daughter infers the plot from reactions of disapproval when she struggles to express her own preferences and her own desires. The more the parents push their scenario on the daughter, the more she rebels and seeks to define herself in counterpoint to her parents' wishes.

Meadow establishes her independence by choosing a man she knows her father will hate. When Tony intercedes, she cuts him out of her life. Meadow's spurning of Tony is heartbreaking because we know that something precious between them has been lost. Sometimes the only way an eighteen-year-old can leave home, of course, is by repudiating parental values and going forth in the world in a diametrically opposed direction. The irony of Meadow's rejection of her dad is that she ultimately ends up with Jackie Aprile, Jr., a carbon copy of her father. The journey away from one's origins inevitably leads back home.

With Tony's son, A.J., we feel a different type of heartbreak because the father–son bond was never established in the first place. Tony has no clue about how to be a father to a son. His own father was also clueless, and most of what Tony has learned about fathering has come from the Bobby Knight School of Human Relations. Carmela tells Tony she read in *Time* magazine about a study that said fathers need to spend time with their sons because paternal support is crucial to a boy's capacity to manage frustration, to master new circumstances and to succeed in school. Tony's response: "He needs toughening up. Someone needs to teach him street smarts, how not to be a sucker, how not to be involved with the wrong people. I don't want another Christopher on my hands."

The irony is that A.J. is becoming exactly like Christopher. Tony tries to instill values in A.J. by humiliating him in the same way he shames members of his Mob family like Christopher. Whenever A.J. expresses any interest or initiative, Tony browbeats him. At the dinner table, Tony and Carmela are discussing Meadow's college choices. She is the golden child; her possibilities are unlimited. Will it be Georgetown? Berkeley? Columbia? A.J. chimes in with his preferences—Harvard or West Point. Tony says scornfully, "The closest you'll get to those places is seeing them on television."

Sometime later, though, when Carmela asks A.J. where he wants to go to college, Tony answers for him: "West Point." A.J.

looks incredulous: "West Point?" Tony says, "Yeah, that's what you said." A.J. denies it: "No way I'd ever say that. I could never get in." Tony completely misses the sad reality that A.J. has given up on his dream partly because his father has shamed him into feeling that he could never measure up. In the worst confrontation of all, Tony points to his son and screams at Carmela: "I'm supposed to get a vasectomy when *this* is my male heir?"

From early on, we know that A.J. is headed for juvenile delinquency and possibly the same life of crime that his father has led. He drinks the sacramental wine at school, and Tony and Carmela are called in by the principal. A psychologist raises the possibility of attention deficit disorder. A discussion ensues: Is A.J. sick or bad? Does he need treatment or, as Tony puts it, "a whack up the side of the head"? This same dialectic surrounds Tony. Is he inherently evil or is he troubled? Is he redeemable or a lost cause? Carmela thinks that A.J. has an illness that needs treatment. At Sunday dinner with Livia and Uncle Junior, new perspectives are introduced into the debate. Uncle Junior says, "Boys will be boys." Livia reminisces about Tony's youth and fondly remembers how she "practically lived in the vice principal's office." Junior and Livia talk about Tony's juvenile delinquency with smiles on their faces. A.J. lights up when he hears these tales. Tony explodes at his mother and uncle for encouraging A.J.

In a classic work on antisocial behavior in adolescents, psychoanalyst Adelaide Johnson commented on how delinquent behavior can be passed from generation to generation. What the parents say about moral values to their children is often subtly undermined by conscious or unconscious permissiveness and inconsistency toward the child in the parents' responses to his acting up. These mixed messages about antisocial acts, in turn, reproduce the way the parents' parents reacted to such behavior. The adolescent may be acting out the forbidden impulses and wishes of the parents or grandparents. At the Soprano dinner table, we see an unmistakable pride in the family tradition of breaking rules and following laws of their own. And when the school psychologist tells Tony and Carmela that A.J. has five of nine symptoms associated with attention deficit disorder, Tony dismisses the diagnosis: "It's a sickness to fidget?"

We all laugh in sympathy because many of us wonder if ADD has become the diagnosis du jour. What is the line between being bored and restless in a classroom and having a psychiatric disorder? Have we become obsessed with placing diagnostic labels on misbehavior? Can *homework interruptus* syndrome be far behind?

Tony is perplexed by A.J.'s rebellion against the teachings of the church. Why won't his son collude with him in his perfunctory endorsement of Catholic values? Why isn't he interested in being confirmed like every other good (or bad) Catholic boy? How can he believe there is no God? A.J. clarifies: "It's not *no* God. Just God is dead." Tony wants to know who said such a thing. A.J. responds, "Nitch. He's a nineteenth-century philosopher from Germany. That's why I'm not getting confirmed." Tony reminds A.J. that Carmela is adamant that he be confirmed. "What does she know?" asks A.J. scornfully. Tony has the last word: "She knows that even if God IS dead, you're still gonna kiss his ass."

Tony desperately tries to maintain the façade of the good Catholic father. A.J. sees through the hypocrisy and voices the same doubts that Tony harbors. As we saw, Tony acknowledges that "the kid's on to somethin'" when Dr. Melfi points out A.J.'s existential dread.

The exchange between father and son is particularly hilarious because of the implicit parody of television sitcom conventions. Imagine an episode of *My Three Sons*. Fred MacMurray is wearing his cardigan sweater and sitting in his study. His son Chip comes in and says, "Dad, can I talk with you a minute?" Dad says, "Sure, Chip. What is it?" Chip says, "I'm concerned that God is dead. That means I'm fucked." Fred MacMurray takes a puff on his pipe and replies, "Well, Chip, I don't think you need to worry about it. Just do your homework, and I'm sure everything will be fine. I don't really think you're fucked, Chip."

The family crises that occur in *The Sopranos* household have much the same form as mainstream sitcoms, but the content is jarring because it intentionally violates the conventions. At the beginning of the third season, A.J. gets Meadow to help him with his homework. He is trying to write a paper about Robert Frost's "Stopping by Woods on a Snowy Evening." The writers work their mischief with the audience's expectations. Meadow asks A.J. what snow symbolizes. He is stumped by her question, so she explains that the snow symbolizes death: "The sleep of death. The big sleep? He's talking about his own death which has yet to come but will come." A.J. reflects for a moment and says, "That's fucked up." As Meadow leaves the room, A.J. calls after her, "I thought black was death." Meadow responds: "White, too."

This scene exploits the academic discrepancy between A.J. and Meadow for maximal entertainment value, but it also leaves viewers with a deep empathy for both characters. The family problems are far too messy and complex to be resolved by the end of the episode, as they are in *The Brady Brunch* or *Ozzie and Harriet*. They are far too messy and complex for easy resolution. Critics have complained that plot elements are left hanging, but the writers recognize that life is like that and have no intention of tying up all the loose ends of the story lines. The viewing public is ready for a darker version of American family life. We have changed. We are no longer satisfied with Pollyannaish solutions to complex family problems. *The Sopranos* is a sitcom for our time.

The Sopranos embeds comedy in tragedy in the same way that *Waiting for Godot* finds humor in existential despair. Tony's relationship with A.J. is also the focus of the most touching psychotherapy scenes. Tony is deeply distressed that A.J. has discovered on the Internet that Tony is the head of a Mob family. A.J. sees the Feds at Jackie Aprile's funeral and

tells his father, "It was like Godfather 1!" Tony flashes back to
the day in his own childhood when he followed Johnny Boy
and Janice to Rideland amusement park and discovered that
his dad was in organized crime. He remembers how helpless
his father looked, and he doesn't want A.J. to see *his* father
that way. He is in a terrible bind, Tony tells Dr. Melfi. He
wants A.J. to be proud of him, but he doesn't want him to be
like him.

Later, when A.J. gets into trouble, Tony looks to Jennifer
for help. He has just buried his best friend's son, Jackie Aprile,
Jr., and he is desperate to keep A.J. from turning out like
Jackie, Jr. Dr. Melfi says to him, "When you blame your genes,
you blame yourself." At this point in his therapy, Tony has recognized the transgenerational pattern, and he knows where
the fault lies.

As a desperate attempt to save A.J., Tony takes him to a
military academy, where they meet with a commandant out
of Stanley Kubrick's *Dr. Strangelove* who preaches the merits
of discipline. Tony wants to be a supportive father, but he
can't help ridiculing A.J. when he comes home and dons his
uniform. He laughs and tells his son he looks like Sergeant
Bilko. When Carmela frets that military school will teach A.J.
to be a killer, she sounds like Peter Sellers's Adlai Stevenson-
ian president in *Dr. Strangelove*, who shouts, "You can't fight in
here. This is the War Room."

The trip to Hudson Military Institute leads to a vicious
fight between Carmela and Tony. "He thinks the world owes

him a fuckin' living," Tony exclaims. Carmela retorts, "What could have given him that bizarre idea?" Tony looks menacingly at his wife and lays down the law: "We tried it your way for fifteen years, with the Berry Brazelton and the validating his feelings. And that fuckin' school did the same thing. And what a surprise! He thinks the world moves on his feelings. Well, he's gonna go learn to be a man!"

The Soprano family aspires to transcend their past while being hopelessly mired in it. Tony is stuck in his old-school immigrant mind-set. Both he and Carmela want their kids to embrace American ideals. But, alas, Meadow falls in love with the handsome scoundrel Jackie Aprile, Jr., and A.J. succumbs to juvenile delinquency. They have become what their parents *do*, not what they say. Tony's fainting spells and panic attacks appear in A.J. just when he is made captain of the high school football team. Generation three, and counting. Old sins cast long shadows.

s·e·v·e·n

THE LOST BOYS

On a quiet afternoon, Christopher Moltisanti is watching television in his underwear, rolling a joint and brooding about his insignificance when the phone rings. Paulie tells him to get dressed and appear at a designated location. He is then taken to a secret ceremony where he becomes a made man. With impressive solemnity, Tony Soprano declares: "Once you enter this family, there's no getting out. This family comes before everything else. Everything! Before your wife, and your children, and your mother, and your father. It's a thing of honor. And God forbid if you get sick or something happens and you can't earn, we'll take care of you 'cuz that's part of it."

Paulie continues: "If you got a problem, you just gotta let somebody know. This man right here. He's like your father. It doesn't matter if it's with someone here or on the outside. You bring it to him, and he'll solve it."

Tony adds unambiguously, "You stay within the family."

A needle is sterilized in a candle as the made men who fill the room look on. Christopher's finger is pricked until it bleeds. Tony then burns a card and continues: "That's St. Peter—my family saint. As that card burns, so may your soul burn in hell if you betray your family. Now rub your hands together and repeat after me, 'May I burn in hell if I betray my friends.'"

At the close of this ceremony, Christopher Moltisanti has entered Tony Soprano's other family. It is a brotherhood of men. As with the Lost Boys in *Peter Pan*, mothers are absent. Whores and strippers abound, but no mothers.

This family is a paramilitary patriarchy. There are capos or captains. There are also privates or goombahs, like Matthew Bevilaqua and Sean Gismonte, who sweep the floor, fetch coffee and do whatever else the bosses want them to do. Orders are issued and obeyed without question. A code of conduct governs behavior. Members of the family do not lay a hand on a made man. They do not disrespect the boss. Violence is only used as a last resort when friendly persuasion fails.

A band of men, most of them dominated by their mothers all their lives, join together in a new family that promises to liberate them from the yoke of maternal power. Lost in an abyss of meaninglessness, stalked by the Grim Reaper at every turn and thirsting for a purpose in their empty lives, these men turn to a powerful father who promises to take care of them. If they fall sick and cannot work, their families will be fed, their children clothed and their mortgages paid.

Viewers of *The* Sopranos—whether male, female, gay or straight—watch these proceedings with varying degrees of envy and admiration: "If only I had friends like that." Chase has observed that "People are basically tribal. I think we still hanker to hang out with our tribe and to be with a bunch of people who . . . at least we say . . . will back me up and I'll back them up no matter what. Also, the idea that justice is actually meted out there. If someone betrays you, you get to have your revenge. You pay. It's satisfying for people to see turncoats get punished." In a time of complex global politics, terrorism and a justice system with 1001 loopholes, the world of *The Sopranos* is refreshingly straightforward. Loyalty is rewarded. Betrayal is punished. End of story.

Although much is made of their manhood, the gang members who hang out at the Bing are more like dependent children under the spell of a charismatic father figure. Freedom is cherished in the United States, but the boys in Tony's Mob family harbor a dirty little secret that most of us share—in our heart of hearts, we loathe freedom. We long to be enslaved to a leader who can magically protect us. If we can participate in his omnipotence, we can believe in an illusion of safety.

In his classic work "Group Psychology in the Analysis of the Ego," Freud made a key point about the need for illusion: "Groups have never thirsted after truth. They demand illusions, and cannot do without them. They constantly give what is unreal precedence over what is real; they are almost as strongly influenced by what is untrue as by what is true." If a charismatic leader tells you to hijack a plane and fly it into the World Trade Center, in return for which you will be met in heaven by a bevy of virgins, you don't question him. Foot soldiers in these kinds of organizations are imbued with the leader's unlimited power: He provides them with the illusions they demand.

The moral standards of members of such a group can be raised or lowered, depending on the leader's character and his personal agenda. The conscience of each member is projected into the leader, who becomes the moral compass for the entire group. The members of the group are then capable of extraordinary sadism and destruction while at the same time feeling exhilarated and freed from moral constraint. Freud noted, "When individuals come together in a group, all their individual inhibitions fall away and all the cruel, brutal and destructive instincts, which lie dormant in individuals as relics of a primitive epoch, are stirred up to find free gratification." Part of the Faustian bargain is a sense of invulnerability. Godfather will protect the family; everyone basks in the warmth of his omnipotence.

The wish to destroy and kill are inherent in the human condition, and it doesn't take much to free up these urges. Observe basic military training, and you will be struck by how easy it is to transform polite eighteen-year-olds into bloodthirsty killers. Little brainwashing or arm-twisting is needed. All these young men need is permission and a cause. Aldous Huxley once observed: "The surest way to work up a crusade in favor of some good cause is to promise people they will have a chance of maltreating someone. To be able to destroy with good conscience, to be able to behave badly and call your bad behavior 'righteous indignation'—this is the height of psychological luxury, the most delicious of moral treats." Men watch Tony and the boys do what they secretly wish they could do—if they could only get away with it.

Thirst for violence is fueled in part by testosterone. Ever since the dawn of recorded history, the male has been the warrior. Manhood continues to be defined by aggressive proclivities: football, boxing, corporate takeovers, political mudslinging or military prowess. Tony, in fact, rationalizes killing by invoking military analogies. He tells Dr. Melfi, "We're soldiers. . . . It's war. Soldiers—they kill other soldiers. We're in a structure where everybody involved knows the stakes. And if you're gonna accept those stakes, you gotta do certain things. It's business. Soldiers. We follow codes. Orders."

At the core of Tony's Mob family is a precariously balanced image of masculinity that must be fiercely maintained to fend off any hint of weakness or femininity that might signal homosexuality. Much of the male bonding among Tony and the gang revolves around contempt and objectification of women, which assures the men that they are superior and minimizes the threat that women pose. The strippers and prostitutes at the Bada Bing are strictly under the control of Tony and Silvio, who manages the Bing. They are occasionally given a slap or two if they are out of line, and they're cut no slack if they don't show up for work.

Against this backdrop of male domination—if not outright abuse—what are we to make of Jennifer Melfi, a powerful woman who won't submit to Tony's rules, much less his sexual overtures? This refusal can only present a dilemma for Tony, which indeed is dangerously exposed when Tony and Jennifer run into each other in a local restaurant. His dinner companions naturally assume that Tony and Jennifer are having sex, and, in a masterful display of macho posturing and homoerotic teasing, the boys waste no time in grilling Tony. Paulie says, "Not a bad ass," and Pussy adds that Jennifer has "world-class blow job lips. Am I right, Skipper?" Tony tries to pretend that he hardly knows her. But the boys are relentless. Paulie wants to know if she was "good or great," and Tony, desperately defending his secret, plays along. "She was good," he says.

Tony is not the only one whose masculine superiority is challenged. Uncle Junior suffers a major humiliation when his longtime girlfriend reveals that he is gifted at cunnilingus. He has pledged her to silence. When she asks him why, he explains: "If you suck pussy, you'll suck anything. A sign that you're weak and possibly a finook" (a pejorative term for homosexual). But ignoring his warning, she gossips in the hair salon, and soon all of New Jersey knows about the peregrinations of Uncle Junior's tongue. To avenge his humiliation, Junior borrows a technique from Jimmy Cagney, rubbing his girlfriend's face in a pie instead of a grapefruit.

In *The Sopranos*, violence invariably erupts when the women question the masculinity of made men in the Mob. And these confrontations are often tinged with homosexual undercurrents. Richie Aprile is embarrassed that his son enters dance contests, and worries that he's gay. Why couldn't he have a son like Jackie Aprile, Jr.? His girlfriend, Tony's sister Janice, asks him what difference it makes. When Richie hits her in the face, Janice retaliates by shooting him.

Tony's masculinity, of course, is also called into question by the fact that he sees a psychiatrist, and especially a woman psychiatrist. Paulie is particularly rattled by this. When Silvio points out that Paulie himself saw a therapist, Paulie protests, "But not a woman. I can't get past that. It don't compute for me."

Performing cunnilingus and visiting a woman psychiatrist are both ill-advised activities that can brand a man as a "finook." During a golf game, Tony teases Uncle Junior by hinting at his penchant for oral sex, and Junior returns the taunt in a reference to Tony's therapy: "At least I can deal with my problems." Tony himself struggles with the feeling that he is compromising his masculine image by seeing Dr. Melfi. When Jennifer tells him about Proust's *Remembrance of Things Past*, in which one bite of a madeleine unleashed a tide of memories, Tony is disdainful: "This sounds very gay," he retorts. "I hope you're not saying that." Jennifer's reference to Proust may be questionable technique (it makes her look a bit like a show-off), but it's hard to see the connection between madeleines and homosexuality unless you happen to be a Mob boss.

The shame of a made man seeing a woman psychiatrist is directly related to the fear of weakness. In Mob discourse, homosexuality is conflated with feminine identification and dependency. At one point, Tony reminds Jennifer of his first visit to her office: "Remember the first time I came here. I said the kind of man I admire is Gary Cooper—the strong, silent type. And how all Americans, all they're doin' is cryin' and confessin' and complainin'—a bunch of fuckin' pussies. Fuck 'em! And now I'm one of 'em. A patient!" In the same scene he refers to "the fuckin' jerk-offs and douche bags I see leavin' this office."

Tony sees psychotherapy with a woman therapist as emasculating. He experienced his mother as castrating, too, of course, so he transfers some of that feeling to Dr. Melfi. In American cinema, this view has been promulgated for decades. By devaluing female therapists as incomplete women who are looking for the right man to make them whole, male filmmakers and audience members can reassure themselves that the patriarchal order is undisturbed. Anxieties of a darker nature, that these professional women might emasculate them, are thus kept at bay.

Hollywood has a particular version of cinematic mythology about masculinity. As Tony says, traditional leading men like Gary Cooper or John Wayne don't talk to women about their feelings. In Lee Tamahori's 1996 film *Mulholland Falls*, for example, hard-boiled cops mercilessly ridicule one of their tough-guy partners when he reveals what he's learned from his female therapist. He's far too talkative to be a "real man," they charge. "That psychiatrist of yours has made you into a piano teacher," declares one of the cops. Clearly, a man who lets himself receive help from a female therapist is a misfit in the tight fraternity of the LAPD.

This attitude is not confined to the LAPD or even to cinematic mythology. Psychotherapists themselves harbor secret doubts about the advisability of assigning a man to a woman for treatment. A study of 170 American analysts found that therapists are reluctant to refer male patients to female analysts. We all share certain biases that are prevalent in filmmakers. The prospect of a woman in power over a man is disconcerting to most of us—whether in psychotherapy or in the world at large. Hillary Rodham Clinton was vilified when she refused to play the traditional role of First Lady and took a powerful position in health care reform. We can't ignore that public outcry pushed her to the periphery and that she gained popularity only in the sympathetic role as the betrayed wife.

The world of the Lost Boys is imbued with ancient traditions and rigid gender roles, which makes the gang's visit to

Italy all the more ironic. In Naples, they eagerly await an audience with the godfather, Don Vittorio. When he finally appears, he turns out to be a demented old man in a wheelchair. His daughter Annalisa (Sofia Milos) is now in charge. Tony, unable to accept the idea that this voluptuous Sophia Loren look-alike is running the show, asks her to introduce him to the boss. When she tells him to talk to her, Tony is incredulous: "A woman boss? Never happen in the States." He doesn't mention, of course, that at home he is beholden to three powerful women—Livia, Carmela and Dr. Melfi (not to mention Meadow). Annalisa comments that men are too much in love with their mothers.

This keen observation from an unexpected source touches on one of the roots of a secret patriarchy like the Mob. None of the guys down at the Bing want to be regarded as "mama's boys." Yet they are all deeply devoted to their mothers, a devotion tinged with worry about losing autonomy and restoring the dependency of childhood. Little boys face a psychological situation different from that of little girls. The little boy must grapple with the fact that his original caregiver is not a male. The child absorbs his mother as an internal presence that soothes him when he is alone and provides solace when he is sad. Little boys identify with their mothers as well as their fathers. The irony of a mobster with the name of "Big Pussy" speaks to the feminine identification that the gang cannot deny yet cannot accept, either.

A little boy identifies with his mother early in life and sees her as his source of food, love and life. But as he grows up, he must establish his independence from her by asserting his differences. Dependency—and love, for that matter—is often associated with resentment, and even hatred. The little boy needs his mother, yet he cannot make her do what he wants her to do. In trying to disentangle himself from her, he may exaggerate those differences, insisting he is not dependent on her or any other woman. The intensity of this position betrays the longing to return to a state of total dependence on a powerful mother.

A female psychiatrist or boss reactivates this childhood dilemma. Tony's encounter with Annalisa reminds him of his relationship with his therapist. Like Jennifer, Annalisa is a beautiful and powerful woman who kindles in him a highly conflictual erotic desire. When Tony tells Annalisa that she reminds him of someone at home, Annalisa tunes in immediately: "Someone you want to fuck. I can tell." Tony, taken aback at how transparent he is, becomes defensive. Eventually he demurs: "Yeah, I do. But I don't shit where I eat. It's bad business."

Tony is not a man of his time. He watches TV documentaries on World War II, and he warns his children that in his house it is still the 1950s. He heads up a patriarchal Mob family at a time when women are coming into power all around him. For him the image of a strong woman conjures up the terrifying memory of Livia threatening to smother him if Johnny Boy moves the family to Las Vegas. As a child, he was at the mercy of an all-powerful, malevolent figure who had complete control over him. Fundamental to the psychology of men is their envy of the life-giving and powerful qualities of the mother. Girls, on the other hand, can look forward to having similar assets when they grow up and assume a maternal role. Men need to devalue their mother in particular, and women in general, as a way of reversing the early mother–infant situation and reassuring themselves of their superiority. For Tony, the ideal woman is one who will meet his dependency needs by comforting him with food and sex, but who lacks any power and control over him. He is unable to find such a woman in Carmela, Dr. Melfi, Annalisa, his mother or even in his girlfriends, Gloria and Irina. As he himself says, they all "break my balls."

Heterosexual male viewers can certainly relate to Tony's dilemma. Each in his own way has tried to find a woman who can take care of him without threatening his masculine position. A divorced male psychiatrist once confided in me, "I'm looking for a woman who will meet all my dependency needs without making me aware that she's doing it."

The old boys' club patriarchy is not the only thing breaking down as the Mafia enters the third millennium. The Mob's code of silence—you talk, you die—is also taking a serious hit. But not before the series' writers can cast a sly look at the lighter side of *omertà*. *The Sopranos* mobsters turn out to have even looser lips than their gossipy wives and girlfriends. Shortly after Livia's death, Tony runs into an old friend, Carmine, a New York boss. They exchange pleasantries, and Carmine asks Tony about his "spells." Astounded by the question, Tony responds defensively. Carmine reassures him that he has no reason to be ashamed, pointing out that, "For Chrissakes, Julius Caesar was an epileptic." He also asks Tony how his visits to his psychiatrist are going. Tony is aghast that Carmine knows about them, but Carmine is philosophical: "So what? There's no stigmata these days. My kid saw a shrink—he got court-ordered for that thing with his wife. They're very happy now."

This exchange was necessary to preserve Tony for the third season of the series. If the Mob didn't transform its attitude toward psychotherapy, Tony would have been dispatched by a hit man long before he ran into Carmine. A plot necessity has been deftly turned into a spoof of the code of silence and of the macho ethos by turning Carmine into the Ann Landers of the New York Mafia.

Of course, breaking the code of silence has a graver side. Despite the initiation ceremony's stern warnings about burning in hell as punishment for betrayal, Tony's pals are singing to the Feds right before his—and our—eyes. The 1970 federal Racketeer-Influenced and Corrupt Organization, or RICO, statute is an important influence on the deterioration of Mob ethics. It allows prosecutors to convict a Mob leader even if no hard evidence links him to a specific crime. If criminal conspiracy can be demonstrated persuasively in a courtroom, the entire gang can be taken to trial. Hence the FBI is eager to find "rats" who will wear a wire and record incriminating details.

RICO and its ramifications play a critical supporting role in the series. Pussy struggles mightily with his conflicting loyalties. The FBI can put him away for the rest of his adult life if he doesn't cooperate. He has three children to support, and he ultimately decides to place their needs over his loyalty pledge to Tony and the gang. The Mob does not take its moral code lightly. Even though the structure may be crumbling, Pussy suffers inner torment and agonizing indecision about wearing a wire and betraying his friends. At A.J.'s confirmation party in the Soprano household, Pussy weeps in the bathroom as he contemplates what he is doing to his best friend. He tries to convince A.J. that Tony is at heart a good man. After all, wasn't Tony the only friend who went with Pussy to the hospital every day to see his dying sister? A.J. is unmoved and comments that "he did all these great things before he was my dad. Now he's just an asshole." Pussy defends Tony and tells A.J. his dad would take a bullet for him and that he's "a stand-up guy."

Tony and Christopher also grapple with loyalty conflicts. Tony makes it clear that he demands complete loyalty or there can be no relationship at all. He tells Christopher that writing a script about his Mob life is a betrayal of his godfather. Unlike Pussy, Christopher capitulates. He knows that he will not find the "arc" of his life in Hollywood. He's become convinced that the film business is rife with hustlers, thieves and backstabbers—thugs far worse than anybody in the Mafia. He has a better shot at heroic stature if he sticks with Tony.

Much of the dramatic tension in *The Sopranos* derives from the dialectic between self-interest and loyalty to Tony. The love between Tony and Pussy, Tony and Jimmy, Tony and Christopher and even Tony and Uncle Junior is authentic. These are blood ties that have lasted for decades. Nevertheless, beneath the surface of devotion and obedience swirls a maelstrom of rivalry and competitiveness. A basic psychoanalytic axiom is that the strength of a defensive posture is directly proportional to the strength of the underlying wish or impulse. Ralph Waldo Emerson was speaking the same language long before the birth of psychoanalysis when he noted that, "The louder he spoke of his honor, the faster we counted our spoons." A minister who adamantly condemns adultery may be defending against his own wishes to stray. In Tony's gangster family, the strong emphasis on absolute loyalty is a defensive posture. The underlying wish is one harbored by every made man—namely to overthrow the boss and become king of the hill. Mob leaders know that the family can be destabilized at any moment by resentments, personality clashes and unbridled ambition.

One episode attests to how the oath of loyalty and the myth of "family" are a thin veneer of civilization that can be shattered in an instant. Freezing and lost in a remote forest, Paulie and Christopher are suffused with paranoia and murderous rage. Paulie threatens to pull rank. Christopher is unfazed: "Captain or no captain, right now we're just two assholes lost in the woods." Suspicion escalates until Christopher pulls a gun on Paulie, who in a state of real fear asks, "All the shit we've been through together—you think I'd really kill you?" Christopher's response is "Yes. I do."

Cain and Abel eventually emerge from their frozen Eden in the garden state of New Jersey, but they have seen the potential for duplicity and will never again drop their vigilance in each other's company. Double-crosses and betrayal lie in wait at every corner in the film noir ambience of the Mob family.

Richie Aprile and Uncle Junior are featured players in this drama of duplicity. Richie courts Tony's sister and brings flowers to his mother. Behind Tony's back he plots a coup. Despite Junior's family ties to Tony, he seriously considers going along with Richie's plans for insurrection until he realizes that Richie does not have the leadership qualities necessary to persuade his comrades. Knowing that he is better off with Tony, Junior betrays Richie's confidence and tips off his nephew.

The metaphor of family in Mob life creates a special sense of pathos in Tony's relationship with Jackie Aprile, Jr. When Jackie, Sr., lay dying, Tony promised to look after his son and make sure he pursued his studies so he could go to medical school as his father so ardently wished. As Tony sees his own son descend into apathy, atheism and despair about ever going to college, he hopes that his relationship with Jackie, Jr., will give him a second chance at fatherhood. Maybe this time, he'll get it right.

Jackie, Jr., however, has internalized his father's values in the same way that A.J. has internalized Tony's. Utterly uninterested in academics, he lies about his studies to keep Tony off his back. He only wants to pursue a Mob lifestyle, and he even offers to do the hit on Tony when he is in alliance with his Uncle Richie.

Tony looks on with alarm as he sees Jackie, Sr.'s, dream crumbling in front of him. Shortly after Jackie, Jr., and Meadow start dating, Tony discovers his godson consorting with strippers and whores. He drags Jackie, Jr., into a men's room and roughs him up for betraying Meadow, his father, and Tony himself. The poignancy here grows out of our sense that Tony is repulsed by the aspects of Jackie, Jr., that are exactly like him. He two-times his girlfriend. He uses charm to deceive his family and friends. He sucks up to Tony while secretly resenting his authority.

Here is the grand paradox of *The Sopranos*. The Mob family is exalted as the ultimate aspiration of Tony and his followers. It represents a value system that transcends self-interest and infuses meaning into empty lives. But the mobsters' children are expected to repudiate the Mob values and lead a conventional middle-class existence. This expectation is, of course, doomed. The sins of the father are fated to be passed on to the sons.

Who among us cannot empathize with Tony's pain? We all look to our children to redeem us. By the time our children are grown, we are fully aware of our shortcomings and failures. Our chance to start over and get it right the second time is gone. Children are our last chance. Like each of us, Tony has raised his children by insisting that they do what he says, not be who he is. He fails at this impossible dream like the rest of us.

A businessman I once saw in therapy agonized about how hard he had driven his son to succeed in athletics because he himself had never realized his dream of being a sports star. When his boy had children of his own, he attended a soccer game to watch his grandson play. His son, who coached the team, spent much of the game mercilessly hounding the grandson to play harder and do better. My patient wept as he told me that it was like looking in a mirror. He had not only cursed his sons by being their model of identification but also cursed the sons of future generations.

Can children ever transcend the sins of their parents? Can they turn out "straight" if they are the offspring of a corrupt father or mother? Of course they can. We all know of such people. But, in *The Sopranos*, the corrupt parents have not been transcended. They haunt these children as surely as Hamlet's father haunted him. They reside as ghosts in the landscape of their children's minds. At each choice point, these children are influenced by the legacy of the past. Indeed, the fact that a child places high value on integrity may reflect an effort to defy the ghostly presence that presses him to repeat history. A morally superior posture may thus be the clearest evidence of ancestral corruption.

Sometimes a compromise is fashioned in which the child fends off the parental influence. But it usually doesn't stay on the sidelines for long. One young man I treated was incensed at the dishonesty of his father, a bookie, who had routinely deceived him throughout his childhood. His father had lied to him about who he was and what he did for a living. To undo the damage, my patient pledged to be "brutally honest" with his own family. But this effort backfired. His honesty was blunt to the point that his wife and small children repeatedly felt criticized. His retort was always, "I'm just trying to be honest." When his wife finally divorced him after ten years of marriage, she told him that his honesty had hurt her and the kids as much as his father's dishonesty had hurt him.

Paulie and Christopher are lost in the forests of New Jersey. Tony is lost in the suburbs of New Jersey. None of them can find a way out of the vortex of crime and violence that they have inherited from their ancestors. But their plight is not merely tragic. The writers emphasize that we are all stuck in repetitive cycles of behavior that may at first appear meaningless to an observer. Consider, for example, the parallels between the FBI men and the Mafia men. The FBI, hard at work trying to bug Tony's house, pose as telephone repairmen and power and light crews. They drive around Tony's neighborhood in vans accompanied by the Peter Gunn theme and

The Police rendition of "I'll Be Watching You." The music tells the story—we're watching the Keystone Kops in all their buffoonery.

While the FBI stalks Tony and his family, the Lost Boys are at Satriale's Pork Store sitting down to a fine Italian meal in the back room. Forced levity conceals the stench of death just below the surface. Patsy Parisi (Dan Grimaldi) can't join in the laughter because his twin brother has passed away and is therefore unable to celebrate their joint birthday. Virtually everyone at the table knows that Tony ordered the hit on Patsy's brother, but part of being a made man is to participate in the deception. Tony begs Patsy to unload his grief and join in the party: "You're with us now. So why don't you leave the morbid shit back at Junior's crew and have a happy birthday."

At a parallel luncheon, the FBI men eat takeout and try to figure out how to plant a microphone in Tony's house without being discovered. They are thwarted again and again as the Soprano family and the Polish housekeeper come and go and by the flooding of the basement after an ancient water heater bursts. When they finally get into the house, they place a bug in a lamp in the basement, only to have Meadow take the lamp to her dorm room at Columbia.

The similarities between cops and robbers is a well-worn theme in crime novels and Hollywood movies. The writers of *The Sopranos* go further by showing us a growing chumminess between the Lost Boys and the FBI agents. In one episode,

Tony and the gang are sitting in front of Satriale's when an FBI man strolls up to the table and introduces Tony to a new agent on the case. Both sides have a congeniality borne of long association, and they chat pleasantly about the bad drivers in the neighborhood and how the Nets are doing this season.

The thin line between the Lost Boys and the FBI is particularly striking in the relationship between Pussy and Skip (Louis Lombardi), the FBI agent to whom he is an informant. The two commiserate about being passed over for promotion. Pussy can't understand how Furio, who just came over from Italy, is allowed to outrank him. Skip retorts: "At least he's Italian. Try being passed over for a Samoan. Three years out of Quantico, and he's the new agent in charge."

Pussy empathizes: "No fuckin' honor. Forget your enemies. You can't even depend on your friends."

Skip offers a sophisticated analysis: "The whole society is fucked."

Pussy eventually becomes interested in crime solving and loses track of which side he's on. Skip has to remind him: "You're not an FBI agent." Skip later says Pussy is the worst case of the Stockholm Syndrome he has ever seen. The Stockholm Syndrome, usually invoked in hostage situations, refers to a hostage's tendency to identify with the captors and to develop trust and affection toward them. Patty Hearst's transformation into "Tanya" while she was held captive by the Symbionese Liberation Army is a well-known example. We all have a fundamental need for attachment to others to assure our safety and survival, even if those to whom we attach are malevolent or abusive.

The Stockholm Syndrome is an example of what psychoanalysts call "identification with the aggressor." The phrase originated to characterize the childhood situation in which a boy must try to become like his father because he is unable to defeat him and take his place with his mother. Over time the usage has expanded to refer to the solution used by someone who is hopelessly trapped and can only cope by becoming identified with the more powerful captor: "If you can't beat 'em, join 'em." Pussy can no longer turn to Tony for his sense of security, so he begins to look to his friend in the FBI. Maybe if he becomes just like Skip, he can find a way out of his tormenting sense of betrayal and duplicity. Of course, Pussy's growing affiliation with his FBI buddy is his downfall.

The Sopranos raises difficult moral questions. Is it more immoral for Pussy to betray his friend Tony by wearing a wire, or for Skip to exploit Pussy's vulnerability by putting him in a position where he's likely to be killed? Alfred North Whitehead once pondered morality: "What is morality in any given time or place? It is what the majority then and there happen to like, and immorality is what they dislike." This observation can be applied to a plethora of situations beyond crime fighting. As Dr. Cusemano points out when he is hosting a dinner party, with the exception of killing people, the same principles used by the Mafia are brought to bear in much of corporate life. Is it moral to convince people that they should buy something they really don't need? Or to increase profits by employing children at low wages abroad? Government continually defines and redefines moral behavior. Is it moral to kill civilians in the pursuit of Osama bin Laden? Or to detain immigrants from Middle Eastern countries? Because corrupt politicians, doctors, clergy and teachers abound in *The Sopranos*, facile statements of moral absolutism become highly dubious.

Pussy's good friend Tony only reluctantly acknowledges that Pussy is wearing a wire. Like the shamans of other cultures and other eras, Tony learns about his Judas from a dream. He contracts food poisoning and spends the night in the throes of a series of fever dreams. In the first, he and his buddies are sitting on a boardwalk discussing Tony's terminal illness. Pussy, however, stares blankly at the sea and is clearly apart from the group in his thoughts. Tony addresses Patsy Parisi, but Patsy turns his head to reveal a bullet wound on the side of his head and clarifies that he is actually Patsy's twin brother Philly, on whom Tony ordered a hit. Tony apologizes. Tony douses himself with gasoline. Right before he immolates himself, he asks, "Where's Pussy?" noting that his friend has disappeared.

In the final dream of the series, Pussy appears as a fish talking to Tony and tells him, "You know I've been workin' with the government, right, Ton?" Tony balks, but Pussy persists: "You passed me over for promotion, Ton. You knew!"

Freud called dreams the royal road to an understanding of the unconscious. In disguised form, dreams often reveal conflicts, wishes and fears of which the dreamer may be entirely unaware in waking life. Tony has been unable to bear the knowledge that his son's godfather has double-crossed him. Yet the signals from Pussy's nonverbal behavior have registered in his unconscious. The dreams, armed with their characteristic disguises, are forcing him to face what he already knows. Pussy, for example, appears as a fish, punning on the slang equating female genitalia with fish. This symbolism also foreshadows that Pussy will "swim with the fishes" when he is unmasked as a traitor.

Tony awakes from his fever dream resolved to avenge Pussy's betrayal. But first he must be certain. When he finds Pussy's wire in his bedroom, his fate is sealed. The code of conduct endorsed by the Mob demands death as the punishment for betrayal. But those who carry out the execution are deeply troubled. They have nightmares. They worry about their own potential for redemption and privately fear divine punishment for their transgressions.

The occasion of Christopher's near-death experience causes the whole gang to rethink their career choice. Paulie provides his own idiosyncratic formulation: "You add up all your mortal sins and multiply that number by 50. Then you add up all your venial [*sic*] sins and multiply that by 25. You add 'em together and that's your sentence. I figure I'm gonna have to do about 6000 years before I get accepted to heaven.

And 6000 years is nothin' in eternity terms. I could do that standin' on my head. It's like a couple of days here." Paulie adheres to a flexible and forgiving view of morality, reminiscent of Groucho Marx's famous comment: "I'm sorry but these are my principles, and if you don't like them, I've got some others."

We chuckle at Paulie's mathematics, but we also recognize a faint glimmer of ourselves. We have to believe in some form of redemption that will forgive us our own failings. Don't we all secretly admire the guy who makes his own rules and gets away with it? Didn't President Clinton's popularity skyrocket when it was discovered that he was receiving oral favors—not regarded as "sex"— from Monica Lewinsky? Indeed, during one of the ladies' lunches at Vesuvio's, Carmela tells her fellow long-suffering Mob wives that Hillary is their role model, suggesting that their husbands and the then president have much in common.

Viewers may think the boys down at the Bing have an enviable life. They hang out, play cards, eat pasta; they operate outside the justice system, which lets them mete out swift and unimpeded justice to those who deserve punishment. No moral relativism here. In the wake of the September 11th terrorist attacks, a picture of Tony and his gang appeared on the Internet. The caption read: "Just tell us where Bin Laden is and fuhgedaboudit."

But Tony's life also has a tragic dimension. Like all of us, he is destined to repeat his past in the present, making the same mistakes, searching in vain for the woman who will liberate him from the tormenting legacy of Livia and finding that his children resent him after all he has done for them. At the end of the third season, Meadow descends into bitterness following Jackie, Jr.'s, death. As Uncle Junior sings the Italian art song "Ungrateful Heart," Meadow storms out of the room and onto the street, leaving Tony a wounded King Lear reflecting on the ingratitude of his children. Like Lear, he views himself as "more sinned against than sinning." He has survived a murderous mother, an uncle who tried to have him killed, friends who betray him, a sister who uses him and children who fail to appreciate him.

Tony has faced his share of monsters. Eleven million viewers feel for him and identify with him. But they also know that he has become monstrous himself and is on an inexorable course of self-destruction. Like Dr. Melfi, we can't take our eyes off the train wreck. Tony could have learned a thing or two from A.J.'s favorite philosopher, Nitch, aka Nietzsche, who said, "He who fights with monsters might take care lest he thereby become a monster. And if you gaze for long into an abyss, the abyss gazes also into you."

NOTES

Chapter 1—Bada Being and Nothingness

page

2   *Warning about parking garage.* Ringstrom, Phillip, 2001. Slate TV Club, May 23.

2   *Unprecedented praise.* Willis, Ellen, 2001, "Our Mobsters, Ourselves: Why *The Sopranos* Is Therapeutic TV," *The Nation*, April 2, p. 26; Franklin, Nancy, 1999, "The Hit Man's Burden," *The New Yorker*, March 29, p. 105.

5   *Heated exchanges.* See the following: Peyser, Herbert, 2001, Tell It Like It Is, *Psychiatric News*, June 1, p. 25; Herman, Barry, 2001, Letter to the Editor, *Psychiatric News*, September 7, p. 26; Moses Ira, 2001, Letter to the Editor, *The New York Times*, June 12, p. D3; Crastnopol, Margaret, 2001, Slate TV Club, March 23; Greenberg, Harvey, 2001, "The Sopranos: Melfimania," *Psychiatric Times*, September, p. 19.

8   *David Chase's commentary.* DVD edition of *The Sopranos*: The Complete First Season, HBO Home Video.

8   *Chase interview.* Witchel, Alex, 1999, *The New York Times*, June 6.

9   *Play space.* Winnicott, Donald Woods, 1971, *Playing and Reality*, New York: Routledge.

11   *Fairy tale.* Carter, Bill, 2001, "Stringing Together Taut Episodes, Not Codas, on 'The Sopranos'," *The New York Times*, July 16, pp. C1, C8.

11   *"Koran" and Providence story.* David Chase's commentary, DVD edition of *The Sopranos: The Complete First Season*, HBO Home Video.

14   *Tony Sirico.* Heath, Chris, 2001, "Sopranos Stars Tell All," *Rolling Stone*, 865, March 29, pp. 42–48, 68–69.

14   *Wiretapped conversation.* Remnick, David, 2001, "Is This the End of Rico?" *The New Yorker*, April 2, pp. 38–44.

16   *"The act is everything."* Sartre, Jean-Paul, 1943/1957, *Being and Nothingness: A Phenomenological Essay on Ontology*, Translated by H. E. Barnes, New York: Washington Square Press, p. 4.

16   *Cast's fear of being killed off.* Heath, Chris, 2001, "Sopranos Stars Tell All," *Rolling Stone* 865, March 29, pp. 42–48, 68–69.

17   *Problem of heroics.* Becker, Ernest, 1973, *The Denial of Death*, New York: The Free Press, p. 6.

20   *Contrast to* Analyze This. Franklin, Nancy, 1999, "The Hit Man's Burden," *The New Yorker*, March 29, p. 105.

20   Heath, Chris, 2001, "Sopranos Stars Tell All," *Rolling Stone* 865, March 29, p. 68.

21   *Our culture's flight.* Willis, Ellen, 2001, "Our Mobsters, Ourselves: Why *The Sopranos* Is Therapeutic TV," *The Nation*, April 2, p. 31.

Chapter 2—Tony's Ailment: Janus in Jersey

page

24   *David Chase's commentary*. DVD edition of *The Sopranos: The Complete First Season*, HBO Home Video.

28   *Brutal killer*. Franklin, Nancy, 1999, "The Hit Man's Burden," *The New Yorker*, March 29, p. 106.

28   *Psychopaths*. Hervey Cleckley popularized the term *psychopath* in his classic 1941 book, *The Mask of Sanity: An Attempt to Clarify Some Issues About the So-Called Psychopathic Personality*, 5th Edition. St.Louis, MO: C. V. Mosby, 1976 (original work published in 1941). For detail about the difference between the psychopath and the antisocial personality disorder, see the following references: Meloy, J. Reid, 1988. *The Psychopathic Mind: Origins, Dynamics, and Treatment*, Northvale, NJ: Jason Aronson; Hare, Robert D. 1991, *The Hare Psychopathy Checklist—Revised*, Ontario: Multi-Health Systems; _____, "Association Between Psychopathy and Narcissism: Theoretical Views and Empirical Evidence," In Elsa F. Ronningstam, ed., *Disorders of Narcissism: Diagnostic, Clinical, and Empirical Implications*, Washington, DC: American Psychiatric Press, pp. 415–436.

For details about the diagnostic criteria for antisocial personality disorder, see psychiatry's official diagnostic manual, American Psychiatric Association, 1994, *Diagnostic and Statistical Manual of Mental Disorders*, 4th edition, Washington, DC: American Psychiatric Press.

29   *Antisocial behavior*. See the following sources: Cadoret, Remi J., William R. Yates, Ed Troughton, et al., 1995, "Genetic-Environmental Interaction in the Genesis of Aggressivity and Conduct Disorders," *Archives of General Psychiatry* 52:916–924; Raine, Adrian, Patricia Brennan, Birgitte Mednick et al., 1996, "High Rates

of Violence, Crime, Academic Problems, and Behavioral Problems in Males with Both Early Neuromotor Deficits and Unstable Family Environments," *Archives of General Psychiatry* 53:544–549; Reiss, David E., Mavis Hetherington, Robert Plomin, et al., 1995, "Genetic Questions for Environmental Studies: Differential Parenting and Psychopathology in Adolescence," *Archives of General Psychiatry,* 52:925–936; Johnson, Jeffrey G., Patricia Cohen, Jocelyn Brown, et al., 1999, "Childhood Maltreatment Increases Risk for Personality Disorders During Childhood," *Archives of General Psychiatry,* 56:600–606.

For recent information about the physiological characteristics of psychopaths, see Herperz, Sabine, Ulrike Werth, Gerald Lukas, et al., 2001, "Emotion in Criminal Offenders with Psychopathy and Borderline Personality Disorder," *Archives of General Psychiatry* 58:737–745.

30   *Harold Konigsberg.* Konigsberg, Eric, 2001, "Blood Relation," *The New Yorker,* August 6, pp. 46–59.

33   *Chase's defense of violence.* Carter, Bill, 2001, "Stringing together taut episodes, not codas on The Sopranos," *The New York Times,* July 16, pp. C1, C8.

34   *David Chase's commentary.* DVD edition of *The Sopranos: The Complete First Season,* HBO Home Video.

35   *Gandolfini on Tony.* 2001, "Sopranos Stars Tell All." *Rolling Stone* 865, March 29, pp. 42–48, 68–69.

36   *Vertical split.* See the following: Gabbard, Glen O., 2000. *Psychodynamic Psychiatry in Clinical Practice: Third Edition,* Washington, DC: American Psychiatric Press; Goldberg, Arnold. 1999. *Being of Two Minds,* New Haven: Yale University Press; Kohut, Heinz, 1971, *The Analysis of the Self,* New York: International Universities Press.

38 *Doubling.* Lifton, Robert Jay, 1986, *The Nazi Doctors: Medical Killing and the Psychology of Genocide*, New York: Basic Books; 1999, *Destroying the World to Save It: Aum Shinrakyo, Apocalyptic Violence, and the New Global Terrorism*, New York: Henry Holt & Co.

40 *Gandolfini interview.* Heath, Chris. 2001. "Sopranos Stars Tell." *Rolling Stone.* 865, March 29, pp. 42–48, 68–69.

43 *David Chase's commentary about the dream of one of his directors.* DVD edition of *The Sopranos*: The Complete First Season, HBO Home Video.

Chapter 3—Tony's Treatment: Flirting with Disaster

page

49 *Essential clash.* Ringstrom, Philip A., 2001, "The Noxious Third: Crimes and Misdemeanors in the Treatment of Tony Soprano and Dr. Melfi," Unpublished manuscript presented at American Psychological Association Division 39 meeting, Santa Fe, NM, April, p. 6.

51 *Freud's analogy.* Freud, Sigmund, 1913, "On Beginning the Treatment (Further Recommendations on the Technique of Psychoanalysis I)," In James Strachey, ed. and trans., *The Standard Edition of the Complete Psychological Works of Sigmund Freud*, London: Hogarth, vol. 12, pp. 121–144, 1958.

55 *Letter to Jung.* McGuire, William, ed., 1974. *The Freud/Jung Letters: the Correspondence Between Sigmund Freud and C. G. Jung*, trans. R. Manheim and R. F. C. Hull, Princeton, NJ: Princeton University Press.

57 *Robin Green's regret.* Dartmouth Department of Psychiatry Grand Rounds presentation, August 2001.

57   *Love in psychotherapy and psychoanalysis.* Gabbard, Glen O., 1996. *Love and Hate in the Analytic Setting*, Northvale, NJ: Jason Aronson.

61   *Casting of Bracco.* DVD edition of *The Sopranos: The Complete First Season*, HBO Home Video.

63   *Women therapists who become sexually involved with their male patients.* Gabbard, Glen O., and Eva P. Lester, 1995, *Boundaries and Boundary Violations in Psychoanalysis*, New York: Basic Books.

65   *Lorraine Bracco's comments.* Symposium at the American Psychoanalytic Association meeting, "Psychotherapy in *The Sopranos*," December 22, 2001.

65   *Chase's defense of the rape.* Carter, Bill, 2001, "Stringing Together Taut Episodes, Not Codas on 'The Sopranos'," *The New York Times*, July 16, pp. C–1, C–8.

65   *Original story line.* Described by Robin Green at the Dartmouth Department of Psychiatry Grand Rounds presentation, August 2001.

68   *Bracco's comment.* Symposium at the American Psychoanalytic Association meeting, "Psychotherapy in *The Sopranos*," December 22, 2001.

70   *Chase's comment.* Witchel, Alex, 1999, "The Son Who Created a Hit, 'The Sopranos.'" *The New York Times*, June 6.

70   *Bracco's comment.* Interview in *The Sopranos: A Family History* by Allen Rucker, 2000, Home Box Office, Middlesex, England: Penguin Books; New York: Signet.

70   *Impact of mother–son incest on adult male patients in analysis.* Gabbard, Glen O., and Stuart W. Twemlow, 1994, The role of mother-son incest in pathogenesis narcissistic personality, *Journal of the American Psychoanalytic Association* 42:171–190.

Chapter 4—Is Tony Treatable?

page

77 *Melanie Klein.* Grosskurth, Phyllis, 1986, *Melanie Klein: Her World and Her Work*, New York: Alfred A. Knopf.

81 *David Chase's commentary.* DVD edition of *The Sopranos: The Complete First Season*, HBO Home Video.

83–84 *Slate TV Club dialogues.* Whitebook, April 16, 2001; Crastnopol, March 20, 2001; Ringstrom, April 16, 2001.

85 *Mentalizing.* Fonagy, Peter, 1998, "An Attachment Theory Approach to Treatment of the Difficult Patient," *Bulletin of the Menninger Clinic*, 62:147–169.

96 *Ellen Willis on Dr. Melfi.* Willis, Ellen, 2001, "Our Mobsters, Ourselves: Why *The Sopranos* Is Therapeutic TV," *The Nation*, April 2, p. 31.

Chapter 5—Medea, Oedipus and Other Family Myths

page

99 *Tony's heart of darkness.* Willis, Ellen, 2001, "Our Mobsters, Ourselves: Why *The Sopranos* Is Therapeutic TV," *The Nation*, April 2, p. 30.

100 *Winnicott.* Winnicott, Donald W., 1949, "Hate in the Countertransference," *International Journal of Psycho-Analysis*, 30:69–74.

102 *Children abused by parents.* Fonagy, Peter, 1998, "An Attachment Theory Approach to Treatment of the Difficult Patient," *Bulletin of The Menninger Clinic*, 62:147–169.

125 *David Chase's commentary.* DVD edition of *The Sopranos*: The Complete First Season, HBO Home Video.

131 *Chase stories about his mother: the snowstorm, etc.* Heath, Chris, 2001, "*Sopranos* Stars Tell All," *Rolling Stone*, March 29, pp. 42–48, 68–69.

106 *Chase on increase in male therapy patients.* Peyser, Marc, 2001, "HBO's Godfather," *Newsweek*, March 5, pp. 54–55.

113 *Mama's boy comment.* Peyser, Marc, 2001, "HBO's Godfather." *Newsweek*, March 5, p. 54

Chapter 6—Scenes from a Marriage: Godfather Knows Best

page

125 *Mate selection.* Dicks, Henry V., 1963, "Object Relations Theory and Marital Studies," *British Journal of Medical Psychology*. 36:125–129.

131 *Slate TV Club dialogues.* Whitebook, April 9, 2001; Ringstrom, April 9, 2001; Crastnopol, May 7, 2001.

132–133 *Green, Ronald,* Personal communication.

137 *Edie Falco has some ideas.* Rucker, Allen, 2000, *The Sopranos: A Family History*, New York: New American Library.

138–139 *Madonna/whore.* Freud, Sigmund, 1910, "A Special Type of Choice of Object Made by Men (Contributions to the Psychology of Love I)," In James Strachey, ed. and trans., *The Standard Edition of the Complete Psychological Works of Sigmund Freud*, London: Hogarth, Vol. 11, p.170, 1957.

139 *Slate TV Club dialogues.* Ringstrom, Phillip, April 18, 2001.

142 *Slate TV Club dialogues.* Crastnopol, Margaret, May 7, 2001.

143 *Bracco quote.* Strum, Charles, 1999. "Even a Mobster Needs Someone to Talk to," *The New York Times*, January, 3.

150 *A.J.'s delinquency.* Johnson, Adelaide M., 1949, "Sanctions for Superego Lacunae of Adolescents," In *Searchlights on Delinquency: New Psychoanalytic Studies*, Edited by Eissler, Kurt R., New York: International Universities Press, pp. 225–245.

Chapter 7—The Lost Boys

page

159 *David Chase's comments.* Interview with Charlie Rose, March 7, 2001.

159 *Need for illusion.* Freud, S., 1921, "Group Psychology and the Analysis of the Ego," In *Standard Edition of the Complete Psychological Works of Sigmund Freud*, London. Hogarth, vol. 18, pp. 67–143, 1955. Quotations are on pp. 80 and 79.

161 *Aldous Huxley.* 1922, *Chrome Yellow*, New York: Harper and Row.

165 *Research on male patients and female analysts.* Mayer, Elizabeth, and D. De Marneffe, 1992, "When Theory and Practice Diverge: Gender-related Patterns of Referral to Psychoanalysis, *Journal of the American Psychoanalytic Association*, 40:551–586.